THE MAUDSLEY
The Maudsley Series

THE MAUDSLEY SERIES

HENRY MAUDSLEY, from whom the series of monographs takes its name, was the founder of The Maudsley Hospital and the most prominent English psychiatrist of his generation. The Maudsley Hospital was united with the Bethlem Royal Hospital in 1948 and its medical school, renamed the Institute of Psychiatry at the same time, became a constituent part of the British Postgraduate Medical Federation. It is now a school of King's College, London, and entrusted with the duty of advancing psychiatry by teaching and research. The South London & Maudsley NHS Trust, together with the Institute of Psychiatry, are jointly known as The Maudsley.

The monograph series reports high quality empirical work on a single topic of relevance to mental health, carried out at the Maudsley. This can be by single or multiple authors. Some of the monographs are directly concerned with clinical problems; others are in scientific fields of direct or indirect relevance to mental health and that are cultivated for the furtherance of psychiatry.

The Maudsley Series

Mental Health Services for Adults with Intellectual Disability

Strategies and Solutions

Edited by Nick Bouras and Geraldine Holt

Psychology Press
Taylor & Francis Group
HOVE AND NEW YORK

BP53

First published 2010
by Psychology Press
27 Church Road, Hove, East Sussex BN3 2FA

Simultaneously published in the USA and Canada
by Psychology Press
270 Madison Avenue, New York, NY 10016

Psychology Press is an imprint of the Taylor & Francis Group, an Informa business

Copyright © 2010 Psychology Press

Typeset in Times by Garfield Morgan, Swansea, West Glamorgan
Printed and bound in Great Britain by TJ International Ltd, Padstow, Cornwall
Cover design by Lisa Dynan

This publication has been produced with paper manufactured to strict environmental standards and with pulp derived from sustainable forests.

British Library Cataloguing in Publication Data
A catalogue record for this book is available from the British Library

Library of Congress Cataloging-in-Publication Data
Mental health services for adults with intellectual disability : strategies and solutions / edited by Nick Bouras and Geraldine Holt.
      p. ; cm. – (Maudsley monographs, ISSN 0076-5465)
   Includes bibliographical references and index.
   ISBN 978-1-84872-040-4 (hardback : alk. paper) 1. Mental retardation. 2. Mental health services. I. Bouras, Nick. II. Holt, Geraldine, 1951– III. Series: Maudsley monographs, 0076-5465.
   [DNLM: 1. Mental Disorders–therapy–Great Britain. 2. Mental Retardation–therapy–Great Britain. 3. Adult–Great Britain. 4. Health Policy–Great Britain. 5. Mental Disorders–diagnosis–Great Britain. 6. Mental Health Services–Great Britain. 7. Mental Retardation–diagnosis–Great Britain. 8. Mentally Disabled Persons–Great Britain. W1 MA997 2010 / WM 307.M5 M54855 2010]
   RC570.M378 2010
   362.2–dc22

                                                                2009046872

ISBN: 978-1-84872-040-4 (hbk)

ISSN: 0076-5465

7/ɔɔ/10

Contents

List of contributors

Titi Akinsola,
Consultant Psychiatrist,
Bedfordshire and Luton Partnership,
Luton, UK

Nick Bouras,
Professor Emeritus of Psychiatry,
Health Service and Population Research Department,
Institute of Psychiatry – King's College London,
David Goldberg Centre,
London, UK

Nancy Cain,
Associate Professor of Clinical Psychiatry,
University of Rochester,
Rochester, NY,
USA

Eddie Chaplin,
Strategy Nurse, MH-LD,
Honorary Research Associate,
Institute of Psychiatry,
Estia Centre,
South London and Maudsley NHS Foundation Trust,
London, UK

Helen Costello,
Research Coordinator,
Estia Centre,
South London and Maudsley NHS Foundation Trust,
London, UK

Philip Davidson,
Professor of Pediatrics, Environmental Medicine and Psychiatry,
University of Rochester School of Medicine and Dentistry,
Rochester, NY,
USA

Anton Dosen,
Emeritus Professor of Psychiatric Aspects of Intellectual Disability,
Radboud University,
Nijmegen,
The Netherlands

Andrew Flynn,
Consultant Psychiatrist (Psychiatry of Learning Disabilities),
Oxleas NHS Foundation Trust,
Bexley,
London, UK

David Goldberg,
Professor Emeritus,
Institute of Psychiatry – King's College London,
London, UK

José Garcia-Ibañez,
Head,
Villablanca Mental Health Services for Persons with Intellectual Disabilities,
Group Pere-Mata Reus,
Spain

Virginia Giesow,
Program Director,
Crisis Intervention Program,
Rochester, NY,
USA

Shaun Gravestock,
Consultant Psychiatrist in Mental Health of Learning Disabilities,
Estia Centre,
King's College London and the Institute of Psychiatry,
Oxleas NHS Foundation Trust,
Greenwich,
London, UK

Duncan Harding,
Academic Clinical Lecturer in Forensic Psychiatry,
Broadmoor Hospital,
Crowthorne, UK

Steve Hardy,
Training and Consultancy Manager,
Estia Centre,
Munro Centre,
South London and Maudsley NHS Foundation Trust,
London, UK

Colin Hemmings,
Consultant Psychiatrist in Learning Disabilities,
South London and Maudsley NHS Foundation Trust,
Estia Centre,
King's College London and the Institute of Psychiatry,
Croydon, UK

John Hillery,
Consultant Psychiatrist,
Stewarts Hospital, Dublin and Applied Research in Disability Group,
University College Dublin Centre for Disability Studies,
Dublin,
Ireland

Geraldine Holt,
Honorary Senior Lecturer,
South London and Maudsley NHS Foundation Trust,
Estia Centre,
King's College London and the Institute of Psychiatry,
London, UK

Henry Kwok,
Head,
Psychiatric Unit for Learning Disability,
Kwai Chung Hospital,
Hon. Secretary, Section Psychiatry of Intellectual Disability,
World Psychiatric Association,
Hong Kong,
China

Jane McCarthy,
Consultant Psychiatrist,
South London and Maudsley NHS Foundation Trust,
Estia Centre,
King's College London and the Institute of Psychiatry,
Mental Health in Learning Disabilities,
York Clinic,
Guy's Hospital,
London, UK

Almudena Martorell,
Vice-President,
Fundacion Carmen Pardo-Valcarce,
Madrid,
Spain

Ramón Novell-Alsina
Psychiatrist and Chairman of the Specialized Service on Mental Health,
Catalonia Health Department,
Girona,
Spain

Jean O'Hara,   .
Consultant Psychiatrist and Clinical Director,
Mental Health in Learning Disabilities Services,
South London and Maudsley NHS Foundation Trust,
Estia Centre,
King's College London and the Institute of Psychiatry,
London, UK

Dimitrios Paschos,
Consultant Psychiatrist in Learning Disabilities,
South London and Maudsley NHS Foundation Trust,
Estia Centre,
King's College London and the Institute of Psychiatry,
York Clinic,
Guy's Hospital,
London, UK

Max Pickard,
Consultant Psychiatrist,
South London and Maudsley NHS Foundation Trust,
Estia Centre,
King's College London and the Institute of Psychiatry,
Croydon, UK

Dene Robertson,
Consultant Psychiatrist in Behavioural Disorders,
MIETS/Behavioural Disorders Unit,
Bethlem Royal Hospital,
Monks Orchard Road,
Beckenham, UK

Luis Salvador-Carulla,
Professor of Psychiatry,
University of Cadiz,
Cadiz,
Spain

Elias Tsakanikos,
Course Director, MSc Mental Health in Learning Disabilities,
Estia Centre,
King's College London and the Institute of Psychiatry,
London, UK

Jenny Torr,
Director Mental Health,
Centre for Developmental Disability Health Victoria,
Monash University,
Notting Hill,
Australia

Kiriakos Xenitidis,
Consultant Psychiatrist,
Mental Impairment Evaluation and Treatment Service,
South London and Maudsley NHS Foundation Trust,
Honorary Senior Lecturer,
Section of Brain Maturation,
Institute of Psychiatry,
London, UK

Foreword

David Goldberg

This monograph is a fitting tribute to the achievements of Nick Bouras, who has devoted his professional life to improving services for those with both intellectual disability (ID) and mental disorder. It has been written by his loyal staff of the Estia Centre, which has been the vehicle for his success in local, national and international service developments.

The Estia Centre was set up by Guy's Hospital in 1999, but following NHS reorganization is now the responsibility of the South London and Maudsley NHS Foundation Trust. The present monograph has contributions from some of his new colleagues at the Maudsley Hospital, as well as the extensive network of international collaborators with whom the Estia Centre has been associated. Together they have been responsible for many of the improvements in services for people with ID and mental disorder, for the design of training courses to improve understanding of ID, some of the advances in knowledge of the basic brain processes associated with these problems, and the improved measuring instruments that have become available for assessment purposes.

All these are dealt with in the chapters that follow. However, even more important than the achievements are the frank admissions of shortcomings, accompanied by recommendations of what most needs to be done in each area. While the aims of care in the community and normalization are commendable, it is disturbing to note that there are still no satisfactory long-term outcome studies supporting one model over another, just as it is depressing to note how many areas in the world are nowhere near achieving the high standards set by the Estia Centre. As the next few years promise to be a period of financial stringency, this is bad news indeed.

Developments elsewhere in the world sometimes dispense with psychiatrists altogether, perhaps identifying them as being responsible for oversedating those with mental disorders. In this connection it is interesting to note that psychiatrists in Australia agree that adults with ID receive a poor standard of care in both inpatient and community mental health settings, that antipsychotics are over-prescribed and that a higher standard of care would be provided by specialist services if they existed.

We live in a time of rapidly expanding knowledge in this area, and the case for specialist advice being available to a community service, provided by health workers who have received an appropriate training, seems incontestable. The achievements of the Estia Centre in 10 short years are quite remarkable, and this monograph brings their work to a wider audience.

Introduction

Nick Bouras and Geraldine Holt

This book is concerned with the evolution of services to meet the mental health needs of people with intellectual disability (ID), from early deinstitutionalization plans to the implementation of community care 25 years later. The primary focus is on the ways that theories and policies have been applied to clinical practice.

The first plans for deinstitutionalization started in the USA during the early 1960s with John Kennedy's administration, through enabling legislation in the funding of ID services. Parallel initiatives and policies appeared in the UK during the 1970s when disturbing scandals in some long-stay institutions became widely known.

In 1981, the then Guy's Hospital Health District commissioned a development group to plan for local services for people with ID. This followed the decision of the Regional Health Authority to close Darenth Park Hospital in Kent, a large institution with over 1,000 people with ID, serving a wide area of SE London and Kent. The proposed plan included all the components of a comprehensive community-based service for people with ID based on the principles of normalization and attracted a lot of interest from service planners and providers. Its implementation started in late 1982 with the appointment of a multidisciplinary project group consisting of a clinical psychologist, a nurse, a psychiatrist and an administrator.

The first priorities of the project group were to re-provision Darenth Park Hospital with the development of alternative community residential services based on community supported housing. At the same time strong ideological and political views for services to support people with ID were prevailing in favour of a social care model. The view was that mental health problems of this population would be reduced when community care programmes were in place. With the implementation of deinstitutionalization, meeting the mental health needs of those with ID proved to be a major issue. Thus it became clear that if the plans for community care and support for people with ID were to have any chance of success, a robust clinical mental health service was necessary to meet these needs. In the meantime the pressure was mounting on the project team to respond to referrals of people with ID with mental health problems living with their families for whom the option of hospitalization to a place such as Darenth Park was no longer available.

Many service planners and providers of community care expected that general mental health services would assume responsibility for the mental health problems of people with ID living in the community. General mental health services were, however, entirely unprepared to respond as they lacked knowledge and expertise on the diagnosis and treatment of the mental health problems of this population. In addition, the funding that had been previously used for their mental health care while in institutions was now diverted predominantly towards social care in the community rather than towards health care.

As community services started to develop, Community (Learning/) Intellectual Disability Teams were created with a multidisciplinary composition and multiple functions, ranging from a variety of social care tasks to highly specialist mental health provision. These teams were not equivalent to Community Mental Health Teams, whose focus was the delivery of mental health care to those suffering from mental illness. Instead the Community Intellectual Disability Teams each consisted of a group of professionals expecting to respond to a variety of problems from social care to primary health care and tertiary mental health care.

The development of a specialist mental health service, Mental Health in Learning Disabilities (MHiLD), for people with ID was chosen locally and was fully integrated structurally and operationally with the general mental heath services. This model was comparable to other specialist mental health services for older adults, children and adolescents, drugs misuse, homeless, eating disorders, etc. The evolution of MHiLD service over the past 25 years is presented in Chapter 1, which presents the significant milestones in the development of the MHiLD service with reference to a series of national policies introduced during the 1990s and 2000s in England and Wales.

With the acceleration of the closure of the long-stay institutions, the service gap in meeting the mental health needs of people with ID became increasingly apparent across the UK. There has been a proliferation of policy documents over the past 15 years. Access to general mental health services has been a steady theme of governmental policy for the provision of mental health care for people with ID. Most recent policies recommended that there should be some additional specialist support when it is required, as presented in Chapter 1. The implementation of policy, however, has been unclear, inconsistent and contradictory, with commissioners overlooking the increasing demand posed by the low volume but high financial cost of addressing the mental health problems of people with ID. The function of the Community (Learning/)Intellectual Disability Teams offered significant support to local services in meeting the generic needs of people with ID such as physiotherapy, speech and language therapy and some forms of challenging behaviours. With such a wide remit, however, and often lacking appropriate skills and resources, many found it highly problematic to respond to the diagnostic and treatment demands of mental health problems, e.g. psychosis and depression of this population. In addition they often lacked links with general mental health services, which operate from different organizational structures. The notion of providing a mental health service through a Community (Learning/)Intellectual Disability Team seems to be a historical mistake of transferring an institutional model into community care. This contradiction remains and, coupled with strong ongoing ideological arguments as to what constitutes challenging behaviour vs. a diagnosable psychiatric disorder, has led to considerable fragmentation of services for people with ID. Influential policy documents have mixed up mental health problems with challenging behaviour in an attempt to perpetuate social care models, adding to the confusion of commissioning and providing appropriate services as discussed in Chapter 2.

As a result, a large number of people with ID have been placed outside their local area because of the inability of their local services to respond to their complex needs as described in Chapters 1 and 2. This heterogeneous group of people with ID includes many with challenging behaviours. The most complex group are those with usually mild ID and offending behaviour with a forensic history and sometimes coexisting mental health problems. An increasing number of people are also recognized as having an autistic spectrum disorder, for whom neither general mental health nor specialist ID services have been equipped to respond. The issues involved are discussed comprehensively in Chapters 1 and 2.

The MHiLD service attracted considerable interest nationally and internationally, and Chapter 3 highlights some of the collaborations developed over the years with colleagues and partners in Europe, Australia, Asia and United States. Though different countries have unique historical perspectives, national philosophies, various service systems and funding mechanisms, nevertheless the principles of mental health service provision are rather similar. In addition to the developments described in Chapter 3, collaborative projects have been carried out in service developments, research and training with several colleagues in this country including the Tizard Centre, the Welsh Centre for Learning Disabilities, Universities of Manchester, Lancaster and Birmingham as well as internationally with Austria, Italy, Greece, Canada, Japan and others. MHiLD has also had a long relationship with the National Association for Dual Diagnosis (NADD) in the USA.

The MHiLD service was strengthened in 1999 by the development of the Estia Centre, a joint research and training initiative of the South London and Maudsley NHS Foundation Trust and the Institute of Psychiatry of King's College London. The concept was to combine services, training and research with increasing service user involvement in all these areas. This is described in Chapters 1 and 8. Several health service research studies have been carried out by the Estia Centre and are critically discussed in Chapters 5 and 7. It is very difficult and complex to evaluate and measure outcomes in mental health services, because most of the mental health care changes and reforms are motivated by political and social purposes rather than evidence-based practice. It is difficult to assess changes until defined systems are in place. Initially descriptive studies were performed to allow greater understanding of the access and delivery of newly developed services as well as of the needs of the local population. Controlled studies including randomized trials followed, and the key results are included in Chapters 5 and 7.

In the past few years remarkable advances have emerged in the diagnosis of mental health problems for people with ID. The development of improved reliable diagnostic instruments and methods that have led to this are described in Chapter 4. Some of these have been used routinely by MHiLD in the assessment of people with ID and mental health problems referred to our service over the years.

Interesting findings have also emerged from neuroimaging techniques, particularly in people with autistic spectrum disorders, in recent years. Extensive collaborative research has been carried out by our colleagues at the Institute of Psychiatry, King's College London, and the main results are highlighted in Chapters 5 and 6. In addition, issues on genetic syndromes relevant to mental health problems of people with ID in clinical practice are incorporated in Chapter 6.

Our understanding and knowledge about the psychopathology of mental health problems of people with ID has also improved considerably, as well as our treatment methods. These are all discussed in Chapter 7.

The availability of specialist staff training for those working with people with ID varies significantly in quality, content and style from country to country and within the same country. Professional training for psychiatrists, clinical psychologists, nurses and other care professionals has been well established in the UK. Most of these specialist training programmes are unique and through regular accreditation monitoring have reached high quality standards, e.g. specialist training for psychiatrists by the Royal College of Psychiatrists. With community care attention focused on training direct support care staff in residential and day facilities, Estia Centre developed a variety of such training programmes for all levels of staff with an emphasis on the mental health needs and related issues for people with ID. These are presented in Chapter 8 together with some evaluative findings. In addition, several flexible training materials in the form of training packages have been produced by the Estia Centre, which can be used by staff groups in their own settings. In addition to the information presented in Chapter 8 on training developments, more details can be obtained from www.estiacentre.org.

The old institutional model of care represented an inclusive system of care providing accommodation, health care including mental health, social care and activities programmes all in one location. The current provision and delivery of care involves several agencies mostly in different settings. This requires a system of coordination of care that is integrated and person-centred. This is not an easy task for people with ID and mental health needs. All partners involved with commissioning and provision of services should ensure that they are well informed about evidence-based practice and as to what the local needs of the population are so as to determine the delivery of service.

An effective mental health service for people with ID should take into consideration the following components as outlined by Bouras and Holt (2009):

- joint social and health services commissioning
- person and carer participation
- involvement of statutory and voluntary agencies
- a baseline needs assessment of the population to be served
- local and national policies
- preferred outcomes
- service specifications
- purchase of services that have the necessary skills to deliver processes that will provide these outcomes
- high level of awareness of mental health issues by direct support staff in residential and day care services
- high level of awareness of mental health issues by primary care staff
- multidisciplinary composition including psychiatrists, mental health nurses, clinical psychologists, behaviour support specialists, therapists and social workers
- ability to provide consultation, assessment and treatment

- provision of community-based interventions
- access to local specialist and generic community and in-patient assessment, treatment, forensic and rehabilitation facilities
- setting in place of monitoring systems, which may include individual and local outcomes, e.g. complaints and incidents monitoring and scrutiny of statistics.

ACKNOWLEDGEMENTS

We are grateful to the many colleagues in SE London, the UK and further afield for their support in the work that is described in this volume. These include trainee psychiatrists, clinical psychologists, general psychiatrists, nurses, administrative staff and managers. In particular we are indebted to Professor Jim Watson, Head of the Department of Psychiatry and Psychology, at the time United Medical and Dental Schools at Guy's Hospital in the development of the services described and to Professor Graham Thornicroft, Head of Health Service and Population Research, Institute of Psychiatry for his continuing input. We are also thankful to Professor Anthony David, Chairman of The Maudsley Series for supporting this publication.

REFERENCE

Bouras, N. and Holt, G. (2009) The planning and provision of psychiatric services for adults with intellectual disability. In M. Gelder, N. Andreasen, J. Lopez-Ibor and J. Geddes (eds), *New Oxford Textbook of Psychiatry* (2nd ed., pp. 1887–1894). Oxford: Oxford University Press.

PART I

Development of specialist mental health services

CHAPTER ONE

The specialist mental health model and other services in a changing environment

Eddie Chaplin, Dimitrios Paschos and Jean O'Hara

INTRODUCTION

Government policy changes over the past 40 years have largely shaped the provision of services for people with intellectual disability (ID). Deinstitutionalisation pushed the emphasis onto community care and independent living, according to the principles of normalisation. This chapter examines the growth of mental health services for people with ID during this period.

The forerunner of specialist mental health services for people with ID and mental health problems is the Mental Health in Learning Disabilities (MHiLD) service in South-East London, which originated in 1983 (as 'Psychiatry of Mental Handicap' at the time) as a response to the need to accelerate the closure of long-stay 'mental handicap' hospitals and to support people with ID to reintegrate in the community. By that time, it had already become apparent that the expectation that community living would reduce behavioural and mental health problems in people with ID was not realistic. In fact, for some people the opposite was true – the 'relocation syndrome' characterised by increased depression, isolation and problem behaviour as a reaction to the move (Bouras et al. 1993) was observed especially in those for whom no adequate planning had taken place.

DEVELOPMENT OF MENTAL HEALTH SERVICES
FOR PEOPLE WITH INTELLECTUAL DISABILITY

From as early as 1996, the Royal College of Psychiatrists (RCP) had advocated for specialist mental health services (RCP 1996, 2003). Day (1993) discussed the need for specialist services for a number of sub-specialities that relate to people with ID; this was in spite of concerns regarding the mix of differing diagnoses that could be counterproductive to positive clinical outcomes. There has gradually been recognition of the increased demand for specialist psychiatric services for people with ID, compared to what was initially anticipated at the point of deinstitutionalization. At present there are different service configurations, from traditional models that employ Community ID Teams to manage an individual's mental and physical health (Hassiotis et al. 2000) at one end of the spectrum to specialist mental health services for people with ID at the other. Although the traditional approach is still preferred in a number of areas, it could be argued it is outdated in that it prevents both integration and inclusion, making it more difficult to access mainstream services from the outset. The model employed by many traditional Community ID Teams could be described as a "one stop shop", just as the institutions that went before. In the extremes these models may have an anti-psychiatry bias that drives a resistance to provide specialist mental health services or have input from these teams. Alternatively other models will operate within a mental health framework with specialist mental health teams, either dependent on or independent of generic adult mental health teams. This includes virtual services, where expertise is added to complement existing services.

In comparison to the general population, recent reviews and research have put estimates of mental health problems at over a third of the total ID population (Kerker et al. 2004, 36% and Cooper et al. 2007, 40.1%). Disparities in service provision have led to an *ad hoc* response over the past two decades, at both local and national levels, as to how best to provide mental health care for people with ID. This has resulted in a mix of service designs offering various degrees of expertise but often without consensus of the wider stakeholder groups, and with inequalities and disproportionate spending on ID services compared to other forms of care (Pritchard and Roy 2006).

Within the UK we are now in an era of systematic audit of specialist services for people with ID. This follows a number of public inquiries that reported a history of abuse and failing services (Commision for Healthcare Audit and Inspection 2006, 2007b). Across the country the reality is broad variations in the quality of ID inpatient services. Such recent disparities and concerns over both safety and quality have led the Healthcare Commission (a powerful health regulatory body in the UK) to call for 'sweeping and sustained' changes to ID services (Commision for Healthcare Audit and Inspection 2007a). The era of audit philosophy has been brought about largely by the direct results of these and other influential reports. However, concerns have been raised as to what audits can realistically achieve, in that they can drain resources from the areas where there is a problem; inquiry reports have mainly confirmed a history of chronic under-funding and limited resources (Clegg 2008). Currently there are providers in both the independent and public sector, with services built in some cases as a reaction to market trends and need within the public sector. This ability to react and adapt to a sensitive market has made the independent sector within the UK the main providers for certain services, e.g. forensic provision.

Within local services, some of the differences and fluctuations to care pathways can be explained by large out-of-area populations in both hospital and residential settings (Allen et al. 2007). The lack of local provision, for a variety of reasons, impacts on current commissioning practices, with up to 63% of people with ID requiring such services in inner London placed out of area (Emerson and Robertson 2008). Without defined care pathways and because of the lack of local services, there is a tendency that practitioners and clinicians become desensitised to the process of moving people out of area (Vaughan 2003), with non-adherence to the central principles of the National Service Frameworks (Department of Health 1999c), the Reed Report (1992) Green Light Toolkit (Valuing People Support Team/National Institute for Mental Health 2004) and the Mansell Reports (1992, 2007).

BARRIERS TO PROVIDING LOCAL SERVICES AND CARE PATHWAYS

It is recognised that access to healthcare *per se* is more difficult for people with ID (Michaels 2008). This is in light of a number of publications, particularly *Death by Indifference* (MENCAP 2007), that highlighted a number of preventable, premature deaths due to failures in the delivery of the current secondary healthcare system for people with ID. A similar concern was raised by 'Closing the Gap' (Disability Rights Commission 2006) about general failings in the primary care provision for people with ID as well as people with mental health problems. Although there is willingness and growing expertise to provide local services, there are still barriers. Arguably the biggest barrier in the provision of mental health services for people with ID is the competing paradigms of mental health and ID services, in terms of philosophical, operational and systems differences. In reality this conflict impacts on eligibility for access to services as well as creating confusion over issues of clinical and financial responsibilities. Compounding this is the new climate of world-class commissioning, involving new initiatives such as 'direct payments', 'payment by results' and 'practice-based commissioning' designed to overhaul the system. In spite of this new wave of ideas there is a dearth of specialist ID commissioning expertise and, rather than help, early indications are that these initiatives may hinder care delivery at a practical level. Other challenges are the changing demand placed on the workforce. As safeguards increase for those using services, so comes the emergence of new and extended roles as legislation is updated, e.g. Mental Health Act 2007 and Mental Capacity Act 2005 in England and Wales. These changes have ramifications for wider stakeholders and also pose questions such as how advocacy services might be provided in the future. The demographic of the ID population has changed over the past 20 years; the changing client group is due to a number of factors including people living outside of institutions and living with families in local communities with increased local expectations, higher incidence of mild ID, increasingly diverse populations with more complex comorbidity and increased age expectancy (Mansell 2007). This along, with the issues of ethnicity and gender, has meant that the need for services to respond to the needs of ever-changing local communities is now greater than it has ever been.

Central to government and good practice guidance (e.g. *Valuing People*, Mansell Reports, Green Light Toolkit) is the inclusion and involvement of service users in shaping and developing services. Within the new NHS Foundation Trusts, service user involvement is underpinned within the philosophy of mutual governance. Mutual governance is designed to strengthen quality and effectiveness of internal and external partnerships, with service users central to that agenda (Monitor 2006). Still in many areas service user involvement across all tiers of service is an aspiration rather than a reality. Notwithstanding pockets of excellence, more needs to be done before we can claim to have effected service user involvement across all aspects of health and social care. It is not just in ID services that user involvement needs to improve, but in the wider health and social care arena. Currently there is a lack of research, monitoring and evaluation with regard to user involvement in social care. Although it is considered best practice there is still little evidence on a national level to inform us of the impact of user involvement (Carr 2004). Similarly in health services, the National User Involvement Project (Joseph Rowntree Foundation 1999), a four-site project that aimed to get service users involved in commissioning decisions, found that apart from raising some awareness there was difficulty in involving service users in the decision-making process. There are a number of reasons as to why this might be, including access and lack of training for the role. Today there is still little in the way of consistency regarding user involvement. A service user network event concluded that to make user involvement a sustained reality there still needs to be more campaigning and negotiation (Branfield and Beresford 2006).

The ability to expand on and sustain user involvement is not always in the control of the clinical team; it is often in the control of the wider organisation. At the Estia Centre an example of an initiative that has been able to be sustained for a number of years is the 'Tuesday Group'. This is a specialised user group for people with mental health problems and ID. This group meets outside of the Estia campus and is hosted within the local MENCAP shop. It meets fortnightly with themed meetings such as mental health promotion and keeping safe. The group's future is protected in terms of being part of the core business planning, and this security has seen it develop to become in demand and active at conferences, local and national events as well as being invited to teach and lecture. The success and positive experiences in working with this group have led to initiatives such as employing members of the group on an as-required basis for tasks such as service audits and consultation events. Other attempts at user involvement have been more difficult to sustain, examples (secondment of a Service User Coordinator and local service user events) of which are described below.

1. Service User Coordinator – This was made possible due to the secondment of a Trust employee for a year who had used services, to coordinate service user involvement and put forward the service user role in developing services. This role helped to achieve a dialogue with hospitals and services in the wider community. The post was instrumental in producing a service user 'Bill of Rights' (Carlile and Dwyer 2005), which was adopted across all mental health services within the Trust and was the result of service user consultation. Unfortunately the post ended with the secondment.
2. Service user events – There have been a number of local borough-wide events to seek feedback on current services (Chaplin et al. 2009). They have been financed by charitable funds.

The involvement of service users in auditing services has been a major step forward, whereas the loss of the Service User Coordinator was a step back. The position offered awareness training, links with outside user groups, induction of users doing sessional work (e.g. audit) and advice on user issues both locally and in the wider Trust. In short it acted as a reminder and conduit for the voice of users in developing services.

With regard to current services, a number of articles have examined different ID and mental health service models. These are mainly descriptive or focus on defined outcomes; length of stay, psychopathology, etc. These reviews have included a comparison as to whether general or specialist inpatient units provided better outcomes (Chaplin 2004). The UK700 Study had a subset of 20%, with borderline intellectual functioning identified within a generic mental health population. The borderline group appeared to benefit significantly from an intensive case management approach (Hassiotis et al. 2001). However, a later study by Martin et al. (2005) failed to show any significant difference between a similar intensive case management approach and standard community treatments (see also Chapter 5).

SERVICE MODELS

How we provide specialist mental health services has changed along with key developments, including detection and identification of mental disorder, a better understanding of treatment modalities and some of their evidence-base and the development of scientific techniques such as neuroimaging. With this has emerged an increased need for training (both clinical staff in a variety of primary and secondary care settlings and community providers of residential and social care services). So far this has been met by a number of centres of excellence attached to clinical services such as the Estia and Tizard Centres. In an effort to provide a measure to help quantify services, Moss et al. (2000) constructed a grid that recorded factors that influence service development. Known as 'the matrix model', it considers two areas:

1. type of service (e.g. national, local or individual)
2. the point in the temporal sequence of service provision (e.g. inputs to the service, the process of providing the service, and the resulting outcome) (see also Chapter 5).

This approach has helped to demonstrate differences in different governments' priorities as well as highlighting cultural differences between services.

Allen (1998) examined services in Wales over 20 years, from the period of deinstitutionalisation, and captured the trend towards community provision. Traditionally with investment in large hospitals, few resources were available for those living at home with families (Todd et al. 2000). The reality is that many local areas lack provision and do not have the number or type of residential placements required for their boroughs' residents, necessitating out-of-area placements. The lack of planning and maintaining the status quo is seen throughout the care pathway, with out-of-area placements seen as viable options in areas that lack access to specialist provision. The move out of area also affects other groups and there may be other reasons than just a lack of local services, such as the failure of local services or family dissatisfaction with local services (Emerson and Robertson 2008). Although community living is the preferred choice, it does not negate the need for hospital admission either for assessment and treatment or in some cases for longer-term admissions for habilitative purposes. This has been exploited by the independent sector, which arguably now leads the provision of specialist services for those who present with the most complex needs.

With a lack of or no investment in the provision of local services in some areas, the independent sector now has a dynamic portfolio that reflects current demand.

The need for specialist services has been recognised as it has become clear that general mental health wards are unable to cater for all of those with ID. Many reasons have been given for this at a clinical level, including complexity of presentation, the need for more detailed or specialist assessment and issues of vulnerability. It is also the case that, from time to time, those presenting as the most challenging to services will have difficulty in obtaining placements in both the NHS and the independent sector. Barriers to developing local services have included a lack of demand, commissioning and provider disputes over local contracts, perceived high costs, and systems failing to evolve through maintaining traditional ideals and working practices. The results are often out-of-area placements, where either the local authority or the responsible clinician maintains responsibility for the individual. This approach is fraught with difficulties in that 'exporting' such cases is seen as the norm, travelling times and costs are seen as prohibitive, and there is in many cases no realistic opportunity of returning for those needing longer term care. The loss of cultural identity through lack of contact has also recently been recognised as a major problem.

The need to provide local services is hampered by a lack of knowledge of local population needs, and agreed outcomes regarding services and service models. This uncertainty can add weight to competing philosophies. Within the UK a number of models have been described, although they have not been formally evaluated over any period (see also Chapter 5). Alexander et al. (2001), in a study over three years, describe two models. The first had designated beds in a general psychiatric unit, which were used for the assessment and treatment of patients with ID across a range of functioning from borderline to moderate. Those with severe ID were referred to a supra-district tertiary care facility. The other model had a dedicated purpose-built unit and catered for people across all levels of ability, and also had access to a tertiary facility. What this study demonstrated was that hospital beds in the second model were provided for service users with severe and profound ID, who would not normally be expected to access mental health services.

Hall et al. (2006) compared community and inpatient services at three points of time for the Mental Health Service for People with Learning Disabilities (MHSPLD). The model uses four beds on an acute mental health ward staffed by mental health nurses with additional ID awareness training and covers an inner city area comprising 340,000 people. The study reported shorter lengths of stay than other inpatient service models. However, with the number of confounders it is not clear whether this conclusion was due to clinical effect, superior care pathways or identification and level of ID.

The model that is now the MHiLD service (Bouras and Holt 2001; Bouras et al. 2003; Chaplin et al. 2008) has been provided for in excess of 25 years. The service was innovative in its concept: a focus on specialist mental health provision for local people with ID within an overall mental health organisation, integrated with a training arm and a clinically directed research/development arm. The service comprises outpatient clinics and a small specialised inpatient assessment and treatment unit based at the Maudsley Hospital. It provides academic and training services locally, nationally and internationally through the Estia Centre (part of the Institute of Psychiatry, King's College London), which also provides awareness- and skills-based training.

The core clinical team includes psychiatrists and community psychiatric nurses. Through its interfaces with other clinical disciplines it offers a multi-agency service with close working with behaviour support therapists, clinical psychologists, social workers, speech and language therapists and occupational therapists. Adults with ID in this model are served through community-based teams, either specialist MHiLD or generic mental health. Those requiring admission would normally go into adult mental health services. If this is not appropriate, for example if a more specialist assessment is required or the person is deemed to be more vulnerable, access to a six-bed specialist unit is initiated. Care is delivered via the Care Programme Approach (CPA) (Department of Health (DoH) 1999a, 1999b). This framework reviews assessment and treatment and helps to ensure effective links with other health and social care services. The CPA framework provides a single care plan that considers risk assessment and management (including crisis and contingency plans), care planning and future reviews.

Although a requirement for those receiving mental health services, the CPA is often overlooked, as many feel it is used in place of a social care process and person-centred planning meetings. This is not the case, as CPA only applies to those accessing mental health services. It is also in the interest of the person completing the CPA that all those significant to the service user are brought together under this process. It can be very much person-centred in its approach, although there may be conflicts in its philosophy. The CPA has been refocused more recently (DoH 2008) to have one level of CPA, instead of the standard and enhanced levels previously. It is anticipated that all those in contact with services will be treated under the principles of CPA. However, it will be the more complex that will have a named CPA coordinator.

Research has found that service users admitted to the specialist unit showed a significant decrease in psychiatric symptoms, an increase in overall level of functioning, a reduction in severity of their mental health problems and an improvement in behavioural function on discharge, and at six and twelve months following discharge compared to those in generic adult mental health services (Xenitidis et al. 2004) (see also Chapter 5). A literature review (Lunsky et al. 2008), found that the populations within specialist units were overall less able than those accessing general services. Despite this observation it is still not clear how people within specialist and general services differ in terms of clinical need and psychopathology. Raitasuo et al. (1999) found that a sample of 40 ID admissions were characterised by mild ID, young males, psychosis and the person having had multiple placements. These findings are not universal. In the case of a specialist service in Leicester, Tajuddis et al. (2004) found that within the two outcome periods studied the demographics of those admitted had changed. In a study of 154 consecutive admissions over a five-and-a-half-year period (Hemmings et al. 2009), characteristics of service users with ID and mental health problems were compared across specialist and generic inpatient units. A significantly longer stay for those admitted to the specialist unit was found. Most admissions to the specialist unit were living with family prior to admission, compared to admissions to generic units. At the point of discharge the proportion of people returning to their families reduced and there was an increase in people going to supported accommodation. In terms of diagnosis those admitted to generic units were more likely to have affective disorders.

CURRENT CHALLENGES

There are changes in the referrals pattern to ID and mental health services over time. This reflects historical, policy and demographic changes, and creates greater demand on the role and remit of services to adapt to this challenge. Resources may need to be reconfigured to respond to changes in the type of cases referred to services.

With a need for specialist services to complement mainstream care, there is a danger that in trying to accommodate this and in an effort to streamline care pathways, ID in patient and community services will become a 'one stop shop' with ID as the defining need. The danger is that such institutionalised practices and approaches will directly impact on the individuals' choice and inclusion within society.

Another barrier is multi-site cooperation: as it is not practicable to provide the whole range of speciality services required in one locality, intra-borough or regional services may be required for some provision, depending on demand.

A balanced model of care for people with ID and mental health needs should include small specialist units where, although treatment in the unit may take longer, significantly better outcomes are reported with service users being less likely to be discharged into out-of-area placements. The proportion of people in the service's caseload with mild ID, living independently and with a history of aggressive behaviour may predict increased use of inpatient beds.

The challenge for modern and world-class commissioning is outlined by the Department of Health, which states:

> It is critical that commissioners are able to distinguish and make appropriate investment in services to meet this genuine need whilst preventing inappropriate admissions to isolated and outdated models of service provision or purchasing services commissioned by other PCTs a long distance from people's home community.
>
> (Department of Health, Office of the National Director,
> Learning Disabilities 2007)

In the absence of clinical trials, there is still today no conclusive evidence as to which service models are the most effective. Further evidence is required before committing resources to a single model of care for people with ID and mental health problems.

CONCLUSION

There is accumulated evidence that people with ID experience mental health and behavioural problems at increased rates and that specialist psychiatric provision is required for a significant minority of this population. Currently the preferred model is treatment through mainstream services and the provision of specialist services where appropriate for those with more complex needs. However, at this time several different models of specialist services are described in the literature, but none with robust longitudinal outcomes. The specialist MHiLD service, operating at a secondary and tertiary level within a mental health organisation, has certain advantages and can deliver high-quality healthcare consistent with modern policies and contemporary service philosophy. This type of model not only provides a specialist service but is designed to complement existing services through its interfaces with both adult mental health and community learning disability services to provide information on appropriate assessment and treatment strategies, but also offers practical assistance through inreach to acute and other general mental health services.

The nature of services means that mental health care for this group will evolve along with developments in training, technology, the changing face of the client group and a greater understanding of the needs of the client group. This requires ongoing service development towards appropriate care pathways. To achieve this there is a need to push the inclusion agenda for people with ID to be involved in developing services. This is not the responsibility of voluntary organisations such as MENCAP, People First, the Judith Trust, or indeed people with ID alone, but of everyone who has a voice, whether they be advocates, friends, carers, clinical and support staff or those responsible for purchasing and providing services.

With regard to current models, further research is needed to establish with any certainty which models of specialist provision are the most effective. The available literature suggests that innovative models that have benefited from longevity, e.g. MHiLD, have helped to take services to the next level with a continued commitment to test current assumptions and ways of working. Although the central component, clinical responsibility to the local community is just one part of the service, along with training and research, to help it play a part in informing the local, national and international agenda.

NECESSARY STEPS TO BETTER SERVICES

- A sign-up for local services that afford people with ID appropriate access to both mainstream and specialist mental health services
- Service interfaces designed to complement the role of specialist mental health services
- Local proactive commissioning strategies that are clear about service delivery for this group
- The use of academic centres to develop the evidence base for this client group
- Further research into effectiveness of outcomes related to clinical models
- Joined-up working to provide partnerships towards joint initiatives such as training to both ID and mental health services

REFERENCES

Alexander, R.T., Piachaud, J. and Singh, I. (2001) Two districts, two models: in-patient care in the psychiatry of learning disability. *British Journal of Developmental Disabilities*, 47, 105–110.

Allen, D. (1998) Changes in admissions to a hospital for people with intellectual disability following development of alternative community services: A brief report. *Journal of Applied Research in Intellectual Disabilities*, 11 (2), 155–165.

Allen, D.G., Lowe, K., Moore, K. and Brophy, S. (2007) Predictors, costs and characteristics of out of area placement for people with intellectual disability and challenging behaviour. *Journal of Intellectual Disability Research*, 51 (6), 409–416.

Bouras, N., Cowley, A., Holt, G., Newton, J.T. and Sturmey, P. (2003) Referral trends. *Disability Research*, 47, 439–446.

Bouras, N. and Holt, G. (2001) Psychiatric treatment in community care. In A. Dosen and K. Day (eds), *Treating Mental Illness and Behavior Disorders in Children and Adults with Mental Retardation* (pp. 493–502). Washington, DC: American Psychiatric Press.

Bouras, N., Kon., Y. and Drummond, C. (1993) Medical and psychiatric needs of adults with a mental handicap. *Journal of Intellectual Disability Research*, 37, 177–182.

Branfield, F. and Beresford, P. (2006) *Making User Involvement Work*. York, UK: Joseph Rowntree Foundation.

Carlile, G. and Dwyer, J. (2005) Giving services a stronger voice. *Occupational Therapy News*, April, p. 33.

Carr, S. (2004) *Has service user participation made a difference to social care services?* Position paper no. 3, Social Care Institute of Excellence, London.

Chaplin, E., Halls, S., Carlile, G., Hardy, S. and Joyce, T. (2009) *Barriers to user involvement in mental health services for people with intellectual disabilities* (unpublished manuscript).

Chaplin, E., O'Hara, J., Holt, G., Hardy, S. and Bouras, N. (2008) MHiLD: A model of specialist mental health services for people with learning disabilities. *Advances in Mental Health and Learning Disabilities*, 2 (4), 46–50.

Chaplin, R. (2004) General psychiatric services for adults with intellectual disability and mental illness: A review. *Journal of Intellectual Disability Research*, 48 (1), 1–10.

Clegg, J. (2008) Holding services to account. *Journal of Intellectual Disability Research*, 52 (7), 581–587.

Commission for Healthcare Audit and Inspection (2006) *Investigation into the Provision of Services for People with Learning Disabilities at Cornwall Partnership NHS Trust*. London: Commission of Healthcare Audit and Inspection.

Commission for Healthcare Audit and Inspection (2007a) *Investigation into the Service for People with Learning Disabilities Provided by Sutton and Merton Primary Care Trust*. London: Commission of Healthcare Audit and Inspection.

Commission for Healthcare Audit and Inspection (2007b) *A Life Like No Other*. London: Commission of Healthcare Audit and Inspection.

Cooper, S.-A., Smiley, E., Morrison, J., Williamson, A. and Allan, L. (2007) Mental ill-health in adults with intellectual disabilities: Prevalence and associated factors. *British Journal of Psychiatry* 190, 27–35.

Day, K. (1993) Mental health services for people with mental retardation: A framework for the future. *Journal of Intellectual Disability Research*, 37 (suppl. 1), 7–16.

Department of Health (2008) *Refocusing the Care Programme Approach*. London: DoH.

Department of Health (1999a) *Establishing Responsible Commissioner; Draft Guidance. HSC Draft*. London: DoH.

Department of Health (1999b) *The New NHS: Guidance on Out of Area Treatments*, HSC 1999/ 117. London: DoH.

Department of Health (1999c) *A National Service Framework for Mental Health: Modern Standards and Service Models*. London: Department of Health.

Department of Health, Office of the National Director, Learning Disabilities (2007) *Commissioning Specialist Learning Disability Health Services: Good Practice Guidance*. London: DoH.

Disability Rights Commission (2006) *Equal Treatment: Closing the Gap*. Stratford-upon-Avon, UK: DRC.

Emerson, E. and Robertson, J. (2008) *Commissioning Person-Centred, Cost Effective, Local Support for People with Learning Disabilities* Lancaster, UK: Lancaster University Social Care Institute for Excellence.

Hall, I., Parkes, C., Samuels, S. and Hassiotis, A. (2006) Working across boundaries: Clinical outcomes for an integrated mental health service for people with intellectual disabilities. *Journal of Intellectual Disability Research*, 50 (8), 598–607.

Hassiotis, A., Barron, P. and O'Hara, J. (2000) Mental health services for people with learning disabilities. *British Medical Journal*, 321, 583–584.

Hassiotis, A., Ukoumunne, O.C., Byford, S., Tyrer, P., Harvey, K., Piachaud, J., Gilvarry, C.

and Fraser, J. (2001) Intellectual functioning and outcome of patients with severe psychotic illness randomized to intensive case management: Report from the UK 700 case management trial. *British Journal of Psychiatry*, 178, 166–171.

Hemmings, C.P., O'Hara, J., McCarthy, J., Holt, G., Coster, F., Costello, H., Hammond, R., Xenitidis, K. and Bouras, N. (2009) Comparison of adults with intellectual disabilities and mental health problems admitted to specialist and generic inpatient units. *British Journal of Learning Disabilities*, 37 (2), 123–128.

Joseph Rowntree Foundation (1999) *Evaluation of the National User Involvement Project*. York: Joseph Rowntree Foundation.

Kerker, B.D., Owens, P.L., Zigler, E. and Horwitz, S.M. (2004) Mental health disorders among individuals with mental retardation: Challenges to accurate prevalence estimates. *Public Health Reports*, 119, 409–417.

Lunsky, Y. Bradley, E. Durbin, J. and Koegl, C. (2008) A comparison of patients with intellectual disability receiving specialised and general services in Ontario's psychiatric hospitals. *Journal of Intellectual Disability Research*, 52 (11), 1003–1012.

Maitland, C., Tsakanikos, E., Holt, G. and Bouras, N. (2006) Mental health service provision for adults with intellectual disability: Sources of referral, clinical characteristics and pathways to care. *Journal of Primary Care Mental Health*, 4, 99–106.

Mansell, J.L. (1992) *Services for People with Learning Disability and Challenging Behaviour or Mental Health Needs*. London: HMSO.

Mansell, J.L. (2007) *Mansell Report 2: Services for People with Learning Disabilities and Challenging Behaviour or Mental Health Needs: Report of a Project Group* (rev. ed.). London: DoH.

Martin, G., Costello, H., Leese, M., Slade, M., Bouras, N., Higgins, S. and Holt, G. (2005) An exploratory study of assertive community treatment for people with intellectual disability and psychiatric disorders: Conceptual, clinical, and service issues. *Journal of Intellectual Disability Research*, 49, 516–524.

Mencap (2007) *Death by Indifference*, London: MENCAP.

Mental Capacity Act 2005: Elizabeth II – Chapter 9. London: HMSO.

Mental Health Act 2007 – Public General Acts – Elizabeth II – Chapter 12. London: HMSO.

Michaels, J. (2008) *Healthcare for All: Report of the Independent Inquiry into Access for Healthcare for People with Learning Disabilities*. London: Aldridge Press.

Monitor (2006) The NHS Foundation Trust Code of Governance. London: Monitor.

Moss, S., Bouras, N. and Holt, G. (2000) Mental health services for people with intellectual disabilities: A conceptual framework. *Journal of Intellectual Disability Research*, 44, 97–107.

Pritchard, A. and Roy, A. (2006) Reversing the export of people with learning disabilities and complex health needs. *British Journal of Learning Disabilities*, 34, 88–93.

Raitasuo, S., Taiminen, T. and Salokangas, R.K. (1999) Characteristics of people with intellectual disability admitted for psychiatric inpatient treatment. *Journal of Intellectual Disability Research*, 43, 112–118.

Reed Report (1992) *Review of Mental Health and Social Services for Mentally Disordered Offenders and Others Requiring Similar Services: Vol. 1: Final Summary Report* (Cm. 2088). London: HMSO.

Royal College of Psychiatrists (1996) *Meeting the Mental Health Needs of People with Learning Disability*. London: Royal College of Psychiatrists.

Royal College of Psychiatrists (2003) *Meeting the Mental Health Needs of People with a Mild Learning Disability*. Royal College of Psychiatrists Council report CR115. London: Royal College of Psychiatrists.

Tajuddin, M., Nadkarni, S., Biswas, A., Watson, J.M. and Bhaumik, S. (2004) A study of the use of an acute inpatient unit for adults with learning disability and mental health problems in Leicestershire, UK. *British Journal of Developmental Disabilities*, 50, 59–68.

Todd, S., Felce, D., Beyer, S., Shearn, J., Perry, J. and Kilsby, M. (2000) Strategic planning and progress under the all Wales Strategy: Reflecting the perceptions of stakeholders. *Journal of Intellectual Disability Research*, 44 (1), 31–44.

Valuing People Support Team/National Institute for Mental Health (2004) *Green Light: How Good Are Your Mental Health Services for People with Learning Disabilities?* London: DoH.

Vaughan, P. (2003) Secure care and treatment needs of individuals with learning disabilities and severe challenging behaviour. *British Journal of Learning Disabilities*, 31 (3), 113–117.

Xenitidis, K., Gratsa, A., Bouras, N., Hammond, R., Ditchfield, H., Holt, G., Martin, J. and Brooks, D. (2004) Psychiatric inpatient care for adults with intellectual disabilities: Generic or specialist units? *Journal of Intellectual Disability Research*, 48, 11–18.

CHAPTER TWO

Services for people with intellectual disability and offending behaviour

Eddie Chaplin and Kiriakos Xenitidis

INTRODUCTION

This chapter summarises current knowledge on the development of services for adults with intellectual disability (ID) with forensic and/or complex needs over the past 25 years. It also details the challenges of new commissioning and policy initiatives. These are examined along with pathways and forensic service development within the NHS and the independent sector.

BACKGROUND AND POLICY CONTEXT

Following the closure of long-stay NHS hospitals for people with ID in the 1980s, there was an increase in demand for a range of local residential and other service provision. Gaps in service provision were seen from the beginning, especially for people with complex needs associated with risk of offending.

Provision for offenders with ID has developed at different speeds across the country. The Butler Report (HMSO 1975) outlined a regional provision of medium secure units. This was partly in response to the vacuum of provision for mentally disordered offenders between the high secure hospitals of Broadmoor, Rampton, Park Lane and Moss Side (now Ashworth North and South) and long-stay hospitals warehousing the mentally ill and those with ID. The new services that resulted from the report were almost exclusively for those with mental disorder without ID. It soon became apparent that the community model adopted on deinstitutionalisation had

23

'forgotten' a significant minority. Policy aimed specifically at offenders has been sparse. It wasn't until 1992 that the Reed Report (HMSO 1992) was published and advocated services for all mentally disordered offenders in line with least restrictive practice philosophies.

Most recently has been the publication of the Bradley Report (Bradley 2009), which looked at the extent to which offenders with mental health problems or learning disabilities could, in appropriate cases, be diverted from prison to other services and what the barriers were to this.

COMMISSIONING GUIDANCE AND MODERN SERVICES

With deinstitutionalisation came the challenge to provide local services. The lack of direction and investment in providing local services for those with mental disorders and ID has come to haunt a new generation, who have not been in institutions but who now find themselves cared for out of area, often in restrictive settings due to a lack of appropriate local resources.

The move to out-of-area placements has led to a plethora of policy and commissioning guidance documents (Royal College of Psychiatrists 1996, 2003; Department of Health 1999, 2007). Although the guidance adds clarity to the expectations and what the preferred ways of working are, there is still no clear national strategy on provision of forensic services for those with intellectual disability. The Reed Report (HMSO 1992) outlines commissioners' responsibility to ensure that:

- services are designed with regard to quality of care and proper attention to individuals' needs
- as far as possible these should be provided within the community rather than in institutions
- under no greater conditions of security than is justified according to danger posed to self and others
- in a way that promotes rehabilitation and chances of sustaining an independent life
- as near as possible to home.

Fifteen years on, the latest Department of Health (2007) commissioning guidance advocating local services illustrates the shortfalls in many local services by reiterating the need to work across agencies to deliver services as a team with:

- links to specialist ID and mental health services
- links and interface with the criminal justice system (CJS), e.g. police, probation, courts and involvement in diversion initiatives
- links to other agencies such as employment and education to facilitate pathways away from the CJS

- the role of the Learning Disability Partnership Boards in ensuring that the needs of those out of area are not forgotten.

BARRIERS TO LOCAL SERVICES

Those admitted to out-of-area placements include those deemed not suitable for mainstream local adult mental health or forensic services. The reasons given for this may include vulnerability and the inability to understand or engage in mainstream treatment regimes. Given the complexity of individual presentations, this group includes not only offenders but also those at risk of offending and who challenge services. Such people often require either short-term psychiatric intensive care units (PICUs) or longer stay mental health units. In the absence of specialist services for this group, services are more likely to have a mix of people with differing characteristics, who may be detained under civil or court sections of the Mental Health Act 2007. In some situations there may be a need to provide more highly specialist care within a larger geographical area where demand is not enough to warrant a local service. In the areas where (either by default or by design) there are few or no local services, funding is complex with many people falling through the gap between current mental health and ID services, demonstrating a need for joint commissioning.

TYPES OF FORENSIC PROVISION

Prisons

Although the aim is for prisons to deliver healthcare as in the NHS, this is not yet a reality, particularly for those with ID. A recent systematic review (Fazel et al. 2008) identified 10 surveys from four different countries that included a total of approximately 12,000 prisoners. The mean age was 29 years, and 92% were male. The results suggest that typically 0.5–1.5% of prisoners were diagnosed with ID. The risk of victimisation and mental illness was highlighted.

For people with ID there are special issues within prison healthcare including vulnerability, difficulties of understanding and engaging in programmes, and access to appropriate healthcare. Although people with ID are often diverted from the CJS (by design or by default) a significant proportion of prisoners have an intellectual disability (Fazel et al. 2008). As evidenced by this review, until recently many prisons estimate the ID population at around 2%. The 'No One Knows' report (Talbot 2007) gives current prison estimates at 7% for an IQ below 70 and 25% having borderline ID with an IQ of less than 80. In Young Offender Institutes 23% under 18 have an IQ less than 70 (Mottram 2007). This has implications for the programmes offered to those with ID, bearing in mind that prison programmes are designed for groups of people who have committed a certain offence and not individually tailored as in hospital. More recently, in another of the 'No One Knows' series, an insight into prisoners' experiences is given (Talbot 2008). The report found a CJS where vulnerable people faced 'personal, systemic and routine' discrimination from the point of arrest through to release from prison.

High secure provision

High secure provision for people with ID is now provided nationally by The National Centre for High Secure Learning Disabilities, Rampton Hospital. High secure provision has remained intact albeit subject to differing philosophical shifts brought about by the Ashworth inquiries. The first (Blom-Cooper 1992) detailed abusive practices through a deeply entrenched staff-centred culture, leading to calls for closure and more local provision models. The later Ashworth inquiry (Fallon et al. 1999) criticised the services for lacking security and boundaries. Following this the Tilt report was commissioned (Tilt et al. 2000). Its recommendations were felt by some clinical staff to focus on purely physical and procedural security, tipping the therapy vs. security balance and making it more difficult to transfer people to lesser degrees of security (Exworthy and Gunn 2003). The report also tipped the balance towards local services, with local trusts being encouraged through financial incentives to move those deemed appropriate to medium secure provision. With high secure hospitals now functioning as national tertiary services comes the need for Primary Care Trusts (PCTs) to consider purchasing this type of provision.

Medium secure units

In recent years there has been a growth of medium secure provision and the limited research there has been has given a fascinating insight into the changing role and development of this type of provision. Alexander et al. (2006) examined outcomes of patients discharged over a 12-year period from the Eric Shepherd Unit, using case analyses and interviews of two cohorts. Cohort 1 discharged between 1987 and 1993 ($n = 27$) and Cohort 2 between 1994 and 2000 ($n = 37$). In comparing these, the following outcomes were considered:

1. reoffending (including any involvement with the police)
2. offending-like behaviour
3. relapses
4. readmission
5. changes of residence
6. level of community support

7. Care Programme Approach (CPA)
8. current statutory supervision.

In terms of ability, Cohort 1 was more able, with 82% having a borderline or no ID compared to 16% in the Cohort 2. Also, there were a greater number of people admitted under civil sections of the Mental Health Act in the second cohort. On discharge it was established that in both cohorts 19 (30%) patients had been in contact with the police. No relationship was found between convictions, previous psychiatric history, ongoing offending-like behaviour or relapse, although those with a history of burglary and theft were found to be more than 14 times more likely to receive a conviction. The study also found that 38 patients (58%) had at least one type of offending-like behaviour and this group were 10 times more likely to have police contact although there was no association with convictions. Long-term outcomes showed no differences in reoffending between the two cohorts although 26 (70%) of Cohort 2 were discharged to residential homes compared to 17 (48%) of Cohort 1.

Early reports from Day (1988, 1994) of male forensic patients with ID at Northgate showed favourable responses to treatment with positive changes to behaviour. The 1988 study reported on 26 patients (six of whom were excluded) with a mean age of 21.4 (range 16–36), IQ range 58–81; six (30%) had suffered frank mental illness, 17 (85%) had a history of serious behavioural problems and 16 (80%) had a past history of convictions. It was reported that those who offended against the person had significantly better outcomes than those who were involved in property offences. In following the group up there was a 55% reconviction rate.

Low secure services

National guidance for standards for low secure units is outlined in the National Minimum Standards for General Adult Services in Psychiatric Intensive Care Units (PICU) and Low Secure Units (Department of Health 2002). Operationally they are more likely to have referrals of offenders, those at risk of offending and those who challenge services, who do not require conditions of medium security.

WOMEN'S SERVICES

In a study of women with moderate and severe ID, high rates of sexual abuse were reported (McCarthy 1999). In spite of such findings the issue of services for women can often take second place when services are planned. There is guidance on building new services with regard to dignity and privacy (Department of Health 2000), but as a group women are regarded by many as more expensive to provide forensic services for. Why this is the

TABLE 2.1
Gender differences in high secure patients

Female patients	Male patients
More likely than male to:	More likely than female to:
• be detained under Part II of the Mental Health Act 1983 as civil patients	• be detained under a Mental Health Act 1983 Restriction Order
• be classified as having a personality disorder and meet the diagnostic criteria for borderline personality disorder	• be classified as having a mental illness
	• have committed homicide
• have an index offence of arson	• have a prior offending record
• be admitted because of suicidal or self harming, behaviour, aggression towards hospital staff or damage to property	• be admitted because of their sexual behaviour or the symptoms of mental illness

case is unclear. Reasons often cited include low numbers, lack of expertise and vulnerability. As a result most new local NHS services being built are for men. Bartlett and Hassell (2001) offer a mental health perspective of why women's needs may differ within general psychiatry, citing:

• the prevalence of certain syndromes (some found more commonly in men, others in women)
• the age at onset of certain syndromes (some begin earlier in one sex than in the other)
• the character and diversity of symptoms (sometimes identical in both sexes, sometimes not)
• the course and severity of illness (sometimes more progressive and more lethal in one sex than in the other)
• the response to existing interventions (sometimes particular to one sex or the other)
• the known risk factors (often distinct in women and men).

Bartlett and Hassell (2001), in examining the characteristics of high secure patients following on from Bland et al. (1999), found the gender differences given in Table 2.1.

In a review of female admissions to Broadmoor Hospital, 26% were reported to have borderline ID (Bland et al. 1999). Bartlett and Hassell (2001) reported on forensic services and found that the majority of women in the NHS were in mixed-sex units (170 women, 94%), while 34 (71%) of the single-sex units were male. Within the independent sector provision was more equal, with 50% of women admitted to 79 single-sex units. In Broadmoor Hospital in the 1990s women who had been admitted were described as more psychiatric than criminal. They were also younger on average than their male counterparts.

In moving services along, the Reed Report regarded certain groups such as female offenders and people with ID as representing special groups. Despite this, the development of female services has been patchy. The move from high security has begun with the new enhanced medium secure units designed specifically for women. However, these are not specialist ID services.

In placing women in secure services one must realise the wider impact on their mental health and families. This is not to say that those needing secure conditions should be placed elsewhere, but rather that these services must be fit for purpose.

COMMUNITY PROVISION

With forensic ID community services still in their infancy, they can often be forgotten when planning services. The reality is those with ID can be disposed of by the courts in the same way as other groups: probation, antisocial behaviour orders, tagging, etc. In terms of community outcomes, the most comprehensive research to date comes from Lindsay (2006), who reports on a 12-year follow-up of a community forensic ID service in Scotland. The study focuses on three groups: male sex offenders ($N = 121$), other male offenders ($N = 105$) and female offenders ($N = 21$). Average IQ for the groups was between 64.9 and 67.5. The study found significantly more women and other male offenders in the younger age groups. In terms of recidivism the female and male sex offenders groups were reported lower than previous reported averages, while a 59% recidivism rate for other male offenders (although in line with prior research) was disappointing to the authors given the uniqueness of the service.

FORENSIC INTELLECTUAL DISABILITY: THE SHIFT TOWARDS LOCAL SERVICES

In looking to develop local services, there is little in the way of guidance and what exists may be difficult to replicate given the differing local service models. A needs assessment of out-of-area forensic patients with ID in the North of England discovered a heterogeneous group with wide-ranging and complex psychiatric needs. Those with mental illness were more likely to be in NHS facilities, whereas those with personality disorder were more likely to be in the independent sector or high secure services. The personality disorder group were most likely to be admitted to higher levels of security, have a poorer prognosis and be associated with more serious crime, and more likely to reoffend (Crossland et al. 2005).

In the South East Thames area 20 low secure services (eight of which were ID services) were assessed against standard 5 of the National Service Framework for Mental Health (Department of Health 1999), i.e. providing the least restrictive service environment (Beer et al. 2005). The study comprised 76 ID patients, 61 (80%) in ID units and 15 (20%) in mental health units. Ninety-five per cent had 0–10 previous admissions, 28% had more than 10 admissions and 41% had spent in excess of 10 years as an inpatient in a single service. In the case notes, 18 (30%) from ID units were reported as non-violent, 4 with minimal violence, 18 moderate, 16 moderate to severe and 4 with severe violence. Length of stay ranged from 1 to 450 months, mean 66.4 months, which was twice as long as those within mental health units. In terms of levels of security required, 18/61 people with ID were assessed by the ward managers as needing a less secure environment. The factors that were felt to be most important in facilitating moving people with ID on were:

1. supervision of medication
2. small residences (five people or fewer)
3. permanent home
4. structured recreational programme
5. multidisciplinary team input
6. trained nurses (the highest perceived need of those with mental health problems).

One of the services within the audit was the Mental Impairment and Evaluation Service (MIETS) which started as a regional service. In the early 1980s, three groups were identified by the South East Thames Regional Health authority (SETRHA) as having special needs:

1. people with severe *mental handicaps* and challenging behaviour
2. people with mild *mental handicaps* and major behavioural or psychiatric problems
3. people with *mental handicaps* and additional sensory impairments
(Murphy et al. 1991)

MIETS was opened in May 1987 in response to the upcoming closure of Darenth Park Hospital, for those who would have the most difficulty adjusting and require further preparation before community living. For those with severe and profound ID and challenging behaviour, the Special Development Team was formed and was community-based. This model of Community ID Teams having a Challenging Behaviour (Needs) team largely applies today.

MIETS offers planned admissions to answer specific clinical questions set by referrers. The service offers planned admissions to answer specific clinical questions set by referrers. These typically included:

*   clarification of diagnosis
*   functions and determinants of behaviour

- risk assessment and management
- medication rationalisation
- development of placement profiles.

The majority of early referrals came from local institutions and reflected the difficulty of placing those with the most complex needs at a time of relocation into community placements. There was also provision for CJS referrals. MIETS's philosophy is rooted in resettlement and integration and its assessment and intervention strategies are based on the evidence base (Murphy et al. 1991; Murphy and Clare 1991; Clare et al. 1992; Clare and Murphy 1993; Xenitidis et al. 1999). Like many low secure services, detention is under forensic and civil sections of the MHA 2007. This is illustrated by Reed et al. (2004), who examined discharges over 14 years, excluding admissions under 8 weeks. Overall there was no difference in the proportions of offenders (defined as those treated under forensic sections) and non-offenders admitted. Of the sample total ($N = 86$), 45 were offenders and 41 non-offenders, with a mean age of 28 and IQ of 66. Using a retrospective case note design, the authors concluded that the non-offenders were more assaultative to staff and to other patients and used weapons significantly more frequently, whereas the offenders group had a higher rate of self-injurious behaviour (SIB). In terms of incidents, offenders had 0.79–0.36 incidents per week, compared to non-offenders' 0.23–0.11 incidents per week. The study also saw that non-offenders required restraint and relocation more frequently, although there were no differences in seclusion rates. The offenders group was less likely to be admitted from the community and subsequently more likely to be discharged to non-community placements, although 71% had a less restrictive placement compared to 59% of non-offenders (not significant). There was some evidence to suggest that patients with ID who have an offending history are no less likely, and may be more likely, to be resettled in the community compared to their counterparts without offending history (Reed et al. 2004).

MIETs has produced a number of publications describing innovative treatment approaches including assessment and treatment of fire-setters and sex offenders and the use of group psychotherapy (Murphy et al. 1991; Murphy and Clare 1991; Clare et al. 1992; Clare and Murphy 1993; Xenitidis et al. 2005).

A LOCAL FORENSIC STRATEGY

Like many areas, the South London and Maudsley NHS Foundation Trust (SLaM) does not have dedicated local specialist forensic services for people with ID. To address this in May 2005, SLaM produced a strategic vision for the local mental health care of people with ID with forensic and complex needs for people in Lambeth, Southwark and Lewisham. With a lack of local services many of this group are placed out of area. To inform the process to develop services, an audit was conducted of out-of-area service users costing £8.8m in placements to SLaM and its partners. The audit was through a case note review and interviews with local care staff. Its findings illustrated a group that were highly heterogeneous and complex in presentation and characterised by a wide range of offending behaviour and mental health needs. Many were found in inappropriate placements with long lengths of stay and at a considerable distance from home.

This audit aimed:

- to identify the numbers of people with ID placed out of area who were at least part-funded by SLaM NHS Trust
- to gain insight into the demographic characteristics of the group, particularly concerning issues of gender and ethnicity
- to understand the offending profiles and clinical characteristics of the population
- to identify the services this population receives, particularly concerning treatments, placement types, and location of placement
- to consider future service needs by evaluating length of time out of area, number of transfers from one out-of-area placement to another, placement appropriateness and future care needs.

The forensic complex ID client group comprised 44 individuals (who had offended or who were at risk of offending) for whom full data could be collected, 32 (73%) men and 12 (27%) women representing almost a 3:1 male–female ratio. There was a strong over-representation of people from a black ethnic background, with 27 (61.46%) identified as such; 15 (34%) were from a white ethnic background and 2 (4.5%) were from other backgrounds.

Referrals to out-of-area services were placed into three categories:

- forensic
- challenging behaviour
- mental health referrals.

The primary reason for referrals was forensic issues, 20 (46%); challenging behaviour was the reason for 15 (34%) and mental health issues for 9 (21%). The majority of service users were full- or part-health funded, 25 (57%) and 2 (5%). Others were funded by social services.

Fifteen (34%) clients had lived in community settings prior to their admission and 9 (21%) had been inpatients within local services. Nearly half were already in secure placements or prison (20, 46%) prior to admission/transfer to their current placement. Use of mental health legislation was evident in the group, though just over a third of admissions were informal (16, 36%). Of the majority who were formally detained, 12 (27%) were held under a Section 3 treatment order, while the remainder were held under court order, either Section 37 (8, 18%) or 37/41 (6, 14%).

In relation to offences, 61% presented with an offending history; assault was the most commonly recorded offence, with 18 (41%). Twenty-two (50%) of the group had no index offence. Sexual offences made up 23% of all offences and 45% of index offences. Other offences included arson (5, 11%), violence (4, 9%) and damage to property (3, 7%), representing 23%, 18% and 14% of the index offences respectively.

The clinical data indicate a group with high levels of clinical need and often with dual and triple diagnoses. All had a diagnosed ID with mild (31, 71%), moderate (6, 14%), borderline (4, 9%) or severe ID (3, 7%). Autistic spectrum disorders were present in 15 (34%), with a small number having diagnoses of both autistic disorder and attention deficit disorder (2, 5%). Psychiatric disorders were also common, 29 (66%) having a psychiatric diagnosis. Psychotic disorder was the most frequent diagnosis, representing 20 (46%) of the total, substance abuse 8 (18%), personality disorder 8 (18%) and mood disorder 5 (11%). Challenging behaviour was present in 18 (41%) of the group.

The overwhelming majority of participants (36, 82%) were prescribed psychotropic medication, with almost a third of these being managed using polypharmacy.

A range of psychosocial therapies were provided, some general, others more specific in nature. Habilitation was provided for the majority of clients (36, 82%), and of the specific treatments behavioural therapies were the most commonly used (30, 68%). More specific cognitive behavioural work was also offered to target particular offence types, i.e. anger management (7, 16%), sex offender programme (6, 14%), and fire-setting (1, 2%).

There was a wide divergence in the length of time participants had spent out of borough (mean 8.41 years, SD = 7.45 years, skewed by one outlier of 41 years). Clients had a mean of 3.02 moves (SD = 2.21) between out-of-area placements. The mean distance of the placement from London was 78.57 miles, though wide variation again was evident (SD = 76.82).

The majority of clients were currently placed in medium-security (14, 32%), low-security (9, 21%) or specialist residential care (19, 43%). Almost half of the placements were deemed inappropriate in terms of level of restriction (20, 45%) for the client based on their current presenting needs.

The audit helped to plot future service development. It was estimated by an expert panel of senior clinicians that the majority of clients required specialist residential care (28, 63%) and a small number general residential care (2, 5%), while a minority would require continuing secure care (14, 32%). The audit also highlighted issues and different types of isolation experienced, including geographical, cultural, lack of contact, with local services, access to families and friends, all of which impacted on the ability to take part in decision-making regarding their own care. Meanwhile diversion of money from the development of local services (either NHS or independent sector) continues, with people placed in more restrictive environments than is necessary.

CONCLUSION

There are few longitudinal studies regarding outcomes of specialist forensic ID services. Those there are offer a fascinating insight into past and present practice and the changing nature of how services are provided, changing patient populations and wider government priorities and policies. This has to be tempered with the reality of a wide range of methodological differences between studies, for example definition of ID, definition of offending, definition of reoffending, lack of external control groups and diverse treatment settings.

The provision and development of forensic services for people with ID has lagged behind mainstream forensic development. There is, however, an identified need for local forensic services across different levels of security, from medium secure to specialist residential placements, evidenced by the large out-of-area populations and lack of care pathways that have often led to people being placed in more restrictive environments than is necessary. In these days of 'world-class commissioning', the provision of local services should be a reality, but in a number of areas this may appear as far away as it ever was.

A small but significant number of people were overlooked at the point of deinstitutionalisation in terms of future planning and provision of services, in spite of guidance. In light of no national direction, different service models have developed throughout the country with no clear strategy. Guidance such as Mansell, Reed and Department of Health commissioning guidance are yet to be achieved. The development of ID forensic services has lagged behind that of mainstream forensic services. Behaviours of people with ID are sometimes not labelled or treated as offences despite being viewed as such in the general population. Audits into services out of area have offered a baseline identifying problems in this area. However, unfortunately in many cases there is no progress in working towards a solution, with the inevitable following human costs.

NECESSARY STEPS TO BETTER SERVICES

- Local forensic strategy outlining care pathways, service, interfaces
- Joined-up working and commissioning agreements with local health and social services

- Eligibility criteria between services that do not preclude access across different organisations along with clinical and financial alignment
- Equity for women in and when developing services
- Links and interfaces with the wider core forensic stakeholders, e.g. CJS, general psychiatric forensic services, prison inreach
- Forensic ID given the same research priority as other forensic services to assist in appropriate service development

REFERENCES

Alexander, R.T., Crouch, K., Halstead, S. and Piachaud, J. (2006) Long-term outcome from a medium secure service for people with intellectual disability. *Journal of Intellectual Disability Research*, 50 (4), 305–315.

Bartlett, A. and Hassell, Y. (2001) Do women need special secure services? *Advances in Psychiatric Treatment*, 7, 302–309.

Beer, D., Turk, V., McGovern, P., Gravestock, S.M., Brooks, D., Barnett, L. and Orr, D. (2005) Characteristics of patients exhibiting severe challenging behaviour in low secure mental health and mild learning disabilities units. *Journal of Psychiatric Intensive Care*, 1, 29–35.

Bland, J., Mezey, G. and Dolan, B. (1999) Special women, special needs: A descriptive study of females in Special Hospitals. *Journal of Forensic Psychiatry*, 10 (1), 34–35.

Blom-Cooper, L. (1992) *Report of the Committee of Inquiry into Complaints about Ashworth Hospital.* Cmd 2028. London: HMSO.

Bradley, K. (2009) *The Bradley Report: Lord Bradley's Review of People with Mental Health Problems or Learning Disabilities in the Criminal Justice System.* London: Department of Health.

Clare, I.C. and Murphy, G.H. (1993) MIETS: A service option for people with mild mental handicaps and challenging behaviour or psychiatric problems: Follow-up of the first six service users discharged. *Mental Handicap Research*, 5, 72–84.

Clare, I.C.H., Murphy, G.H., Cox, D. and Chaplin, E.H. (1992) Assessment and treatment of fire-setting: A single case investigation using a cognitive behavioural model. *Criminal Behaviour and Mental Health*, 2, 253–268.

Crossland, S., Burns, M., Leach, C. and Quinn, P. (2005). Needs assessment in forensic learning disability. *Medicine, Science and the Law*, 45 (2), 147–153.

Day, K. (1988) Male mentally handicapped sex offenders. *British Journal of Psychiatry*, 165, 630–639.

Day, K. (1994) A hospital based treatment programme for male mentally handicapped offenders. *British Journal of Psychiatry*, 153, 635–644.

Department of Health (1999) The *New NHS: Guidance on Out of Area Treatments*, HSC 1999/117. London: Department of Health.

Department of Health (2000) *Privacy, Dignity and Safety in Mental Health Units.* London: Department of Health.

Department of Health (2002) *National Minimum Standards for General Adult Services in Psychiatric Intensive Care Units (PICU) and Low Secure Units.* London: Department of Health.

Department of Health (2007) *Commissioning Specialist Adult Learning Disability Health Services: Good Practice Guidance.* London: Department of Health.

Exworthy, T. and Gunn, J. (2003) Editorial: Taking another tilt at high secure hospitals: The Tilt Report and its consequences for secure psychiatric services. *British Journal of Psychiatry*, 182, 469–471.

Fallon, P., Bluglass, R., Edwards, B. and Daniels, G. (1999) *Report of the Committee of Inquiry into the Personality Disorder Unit, Ashworth Special Hospital* (vol. 1) (Cm 4194, II). London: Stationery Office.

Fazel, S., Xenitidis, K. and Powell, J. (2008) The prevalence of intellectual disabilities among 12 000 prisoners: A systematic review. *International Journal of Law and Psychiatry*, 31 (4), 369–373.

HMSO (1975) *Butler Report, Report of the Committee on Mentally Abnormal Offenders.* London: HMSO.

HMSO (1992) *Reed Report, Review of Mental Health and Social Services for Mentally Disordered Offenders and Others Requiring Similar Services: Vol. 1: Final Summary Report (Cm. 2088).* London: HMSO.

Lindsay, W.R. (2006) A community forensic intellectual disability service: Twelve year follow up of referrals; analysis of referral patterns and assessment of harm reduction. *Legal and Criminological Psychology*, 11 (1), 113–130.

McCarthy, M. (1999) *Sexuality and Women with Learning Disabilities.* London: Jessica Kingsley.

Mottram, P.G. (2007) *HMP: Liverpool, Styall and Hindley Study Report* (vol. 2). University of Liverpool.

Murphy, G.H. and Clare, I.C.H. (1991) MIETS: A service option for people with mild mental handicaps and challenging behaviour or psychiatric problems. Assessment, treatment and outcome for service users and service effectiveness. *Mental Handicap Research*, 4, 180–206.

Murphy, G.H., Holland, A.J., Fowler, P. and Reep, J. (1991) MIETS: A service option for people with mild mental handicaps and challenging behaviour or psychiatric problems 1. Philosophy service and service users. *Mental Handicap Research*, 4, 41–66.

Royal College of Psychiatrists (1996) *Meeting the Mental Health Needs of People with Learning Disability.* London: Royal College of Psychiatrists.

Royal College of Psychiatrists (2003) *Meeting the Mental Health Needs of People with a Mild Learning Disability.* London: Royal College of Psychiatrists Council report CR115.

Talbot, J. (2007) *No One Knows: Identifying and Supporting Prisoners with Learning Difficulties and Learning Disabilities: The Views of Prison Staff.* London: Prison Reform Trust.

Talbot, J. (2008) *No One Knows Report and Final Recommendations: Prisoners' Voices. Experiences of the Criminal Justice System by Prisoners with Learning Disabilities and Difficulties.* London: Prison Reform Trust.

Tilt, R., Perry, B., Martin, C., Maguire, N. and Preston, M. (2000) *Report of the Review of Security at the High Security Hospitals.* London: Department of Health.

Reed, S., Russell, A.J., Xenitidis, K. and Murphy, D.G.M. (2004) People with learning disabilities in a low secure in-patient unit: Comparison of offenders and non offenders. *British Journal of Psychiatry*, 85, 499–504.

Xenitidis, K., Barnes, J. and White, J. (2005) Forensic psychotherapy for adults with learning disabilities: An inpatient group-analytic group. *Group Analysis* 38, 427–438.

Xenitidis, K.I., Henry, J., Russell, A.J., Ward, A. and Murphy, D.G. (1999) An in-patient treatment model for adults with mild intellectual disability and challenging behaviour. *Journal of Intellectual Disability Research*, 43, 128–134.

CHAPTER THREE

An international perspective of mental health services for people with intellectual disability

Nancy Cain (USA), Philip Davidson (USA), Anton Dosen (The Netherlands), José Garcia-Ibañez (Spain), Virginia Giesow (USA), John Hillery (Ireland), Henry Kwok (Hong Kong), Almudena Martorell (Spain), Ramón Novell-Alsina (Spain), Luis Salvador-Carulla (Spain) and Jenny Torr (Australia)

INTRODUCTION

Internationally the trend in the direction of community integration has seen a move towards specialist community facilities and in-patient services for people with ID and mental health problems (Davidson and O'Hara 2007). The Mental Health in Learning Disabilities (MHiLD) Service and Estia Centre through their training, research and service development activities have collaborated with partners across several parts of the world to address the challenges that this brings to service providers. Some of our major partners have contributed to this chapter. They highlight the need to work in collaboration, to share knowledge and expertise and research ideas at a global level, to help shape and develop specialist mental health services for the benefit of all individuals with ID wherever they may be.

Although there is common ground within services in Europe, Australasia, the Americas and parts of Asia, there are marked differences in the development of services and where countries are in regard to achieving community-focused care. A comparison study between five European countries has shown that at an international level, there is considerable variation in quality and type of service provision for people with ID and mental health problems (Holt et al. 2000). Partly this is because of historical reasons to do with political and policy initiatives. In the USA the movement towards services built around people has grown out of the landmark Presidential Panel for people with ID in 1961 (whose initial report,

Combating Mental Retardation (Kennedy 1961) sought to include people with ID in everyday society). This philosophy of care was reiterated in 2004 through the New Freedom Initiative and the *Report to the President: A Charge We Have to Keep: A Road Map to Personal and Economic Freedom for Persons with Intellectual Disabilities* (President's Committee for People with Intellectual Disabilities 2004). How services are shaped is affected by competing paradigms; for example, within Australian policy, tensions are reported between the notions of how disability affects the individual and how society sees the individual and accommodates them, with the majority living in the community with family (Bigby and Ozanne 2001). Within Asia a survey of 14 countries found a wide variation of services, the type of service relating to wider economic and social considerations (Kwok and Chui 2008).

Disparity of service provision also exists between different regions of the same country where local pressures and resources have dictated service developments. Variation across continents and between services exists on a number of levels. These include:

- service design
- care packages
- funding streams
- commissioning
- staffing patterns
- resources.

These issues are further explored now with some of MHiLD and Estia Centre major collaborators from some other countries across the world.

REPUBLIC OF IRELAND

This interplay of national and local factors shaping a patchwork of service development even within one country is exemplified by the situation in the Republic of Ireland.

Historical context

Services for people with ID in Ireland developed from the mid-1800s onwards. Provided by Protestant philanthropists and Catholic religious orders, these were institutionally based and formed the structure on which current services are financed and delivered. People with ID also were placed in psychiatric hospitals. This was common until relatively recently. In recent decades much money has been set aside for resettlement of long-stay psychiatric patients who have no mental illness. In the 1960s schools and community-based residential services were established by so-called 'parents and friends' groups. Such services became a template for the deinstitution-alisation and normalisation in the community of the more traditional campus-based services.

Services today

Today, with a few exceptions, services are community-based in whole or in part, with aspirations to close old campuses and move totally to the community. The medical services to the institutions were provided by doctors with psychiatric training. These doctors tended to have a wide remit beyond mental health issues including general health issues and epilepsy. The newer 'parents and friends' type model of development tends not to have psychiatrists in such positions. This has led to the current situation where many ID services have one or more psychiatrists while some have none at all. The psychiatrists usually treat people who attend the ID services and tend not to have a working relationship with the generic catchment area psychiatric services. If they are working with a multidisciplinary team, it is usually a generic ID team with no members, other than the psychiatrist, with specialist training in mental health and with no members designated to specialise in mental health issues. This has led to deficits in service provision (Royal College of Psychiatrists 2004). It can be very difficult for patients or, indeed, psychiatrists to access the resources needed for appropriate multi-modal assessment and intervention.

The research and practical experience of the MHiLD Service and Estia Centre have informed services in a number of countries (Chapters 1, 5 and 8 of this volume), including recent activities and policy developments in Ireland. The policy document on mental health services produced in 2006 by an expert group appointed by the government, *A Vision for Change* (Department of Health and Children 2006) attempts to rectify the deficits in mental health services and gives special attention to the needs of people with ID. An asset to the planning process in Ireland is the availability of a resourced and regularly updated database of people with ID (the National Intellectual Disability Database, NIDD). This is maintained by the Health Research Board (www.hrb.ie). There are however no figures for the pre-valence of mental illness in people with ID in the Republic of Ireland.

Using data from the NIDD, the expert group proposed recommenda-tions for meeting the mental health needs of people with ID. These included promotion and maintenance of mental well-being as an integral part of service provision in ID services; catchment area-based specialist mental health of ID teams (two per 300,000 population for adults, one per 300,000 for children and adolescents); a spectrum of facilities to provide a flexible continuum of care based on need (five acute in-patient beds and 10 day hospital places per 300,000 as well as rehabilitation and continuing care beds); and services to meet specific groups such as those with mild ID, those with autism and those in the 'forensic population'. The Health Service Executive – the national body responsible for planning and funding all publicly funded health services – has initiated a number of pilot projects based on these proposals.

The attitude to the mental health needs of people with ID has evolved greatly in the Republic of Ireland over the past 20 years, with concrete progress being made in the past few years. There is an obvious acknowledgment of the special needs of this group of the population. There are plans that form part of national policy which, if implemented, will make a great difference to the lives of people with ID and their families and carers. Unfortunately, the current downturn in the world and national economy may jeopardise the implementation of these plans and policies.

THE NETHERLANDS

Historical context

In the Netherlands the differentiation between mental illness and ID dates from the second half of the nineteenth century. However, until the 1950s, institutions for housing people with ID were a rarity. Most individuals with ID were living in family homes or were placed in psychiatric hospitals. In the 1960s, the ideology of 'normalisation' influenced policy for community care. Developmental and educational models of care prevailed for people with ID. Psychiatrists distanced themselves from the care of people with ID while psychology, pedagogy, social work and nursing took the lead. There was little interest in or recognition of the mental health needs of this population.

With the implementation of deinstitutionalisation in the 1970s and 1980s, behavioural and mental health problems became visible. Initially, social care models were used by the non-psychiatric professionals, but the severity of the problems prompted them to request the input of psychiatrists. In this way, during the 1980s, many people with ID made their re-entry into psychiatry. The dilemma was whether to provide generic or specialised mental health services as in other western countries (Bouras and Holt 2001).

In the early 1980s, special clinical centres for adults with ID and severe behaviour disorders were established. Five centres accommodating some 150 in-patients in five country districts were set up, each centre serving an area of three million inhabitants. These centres cater for people with an IQ of 50–90. This broad eligibility criterion is different to other international models, many of which have an upper cut-off at IQ 70. Patients are treated for up to three years and, after treatment, returned to their former milieu. No facilities of this sort were made available for people with moderate and more severe ID. However, a number of centres had already been set up for the observation and treatment of children and adolescents with mild ID and behavioural problems.

The positive effects of these centres became visible within a relatively short period of time. People with severe and chronic psychiatric and behavioural problems, who were not served adequately by general psychiatry, could be assessed and treated properly in these centres. Specialist knowledge within multidisciplinary teams and research increased among young psychiatrists and other professionals for this population.

However, soon it became apparent that these centres were only a temporary solution for a larger problem. The centres provided exclusively in-patient treatment, waiting lists for admission became too long, aftercare was not well organised, and people with moderate and severe ID were excluded.

Services today

At the beginning of the 1990s some in-patient centres developed community outreach multi-professional teams to provide mental health interventions within the living milieu of people with ID. A few general psychiatric hospitals started specialised departments for the assessment and treatment of people with ID. In parallel a professorship in the psychiatric aspects of ID at the Radboud University in Nijmegen was established, which together with the European Association for Mental Health in ID, based in the Netherlands, advocated for specialised services for those with mental health problems and ID.

Some structural changes were implemented in the early 2000s to bring specialist services for people with ID closer to generic mental heath services. These changes enhanced further staff training possibilities, and the number of psychiatrists working in this field of ID has significantly increased (Dosen 2005). Training for psychologists, pedagogues, social workers and nurses has also been improved.

Recent service developments have contributed to breaking down some historical barriers in this field. The most severe barrier was ignorance about the special needs of this population with respect to their mental health, and of the need for specialist knowledge concerning psychiatric diagnostics and treatment of these people (Bouras et al. 1993). One of the barriers was a gap between the two care systems, one for those with ID and another system for mental health care for the general population. Participation of professionals from one system in the other, sharing of professional knowledge and cooperation in care provision offer a solid base for the future development of a real and all-embracing mental health care system for this population.

SPAIN

Historical context

The interest in the mental health of those with ID started early in Spain. In 1969 a group of clinical experts including adult psychiatrists, child psychiatrists, psychologists and stakeholders founded the Spanish Association of Scientific Research in Mental Retardation.

This association was quite influential and was supported by other key organisations in the field such as the Spanish Federation of Family Associations of People with ID. Unfortunately this development came to a halt in the late 1970s because of the relatively low interest of the health care sector including psychiatric services in ID, the increasing interest of clinicians in other areas of psychiatry such as ageing and child psychiatry, and the progressive shift of ID care from the health sector into social and education sectors. This shift increased in the mid-1980s with deinstitutionalisation. The 1986 Health Act included mental health as an area of importance but it did not mention ID, as it was considered mainly a social problem and was excluded from the health care system and from the academic curriculum in medicine and clinical psychology.

During the 1980s, the education sector integrated children with ID into mainstream schools, and the national social care agency together with regional and local NGOs developed a successful network of residential, training and employment programmes. By the 1990s many people with ID had been moved from psychiatric institutions into the community and to residential facilities under the social care sector. By then, stakeholders, families and family associations realised that there was a significant proportion of people with ID who needed psychiatric care.

In the early 1990s only a few psychiatrists were actively involved in the care of people with ID in Spain. They were in the public health system, NGOs, institutional care, and the social care system. However, there was lack of knowledge and skills in diagnostic and treatment methods and specialist training.

In 1989, Dr Juan Perez-Marín, president of one of the main NGOs providing care for people with ID in Spain, invited Professor Luis Salvador-Carulla (University of Cadiz) to assist with service developments for people with ID and mental health problems in Andalucía. A long-lasting collaboration started with MHiLD service and Estia Centre for service developments, training and evaluative research in Spain (Salvador-Carulla and Martínez-Maroto 1993).

Services today

Although there are large regional differences, specialised services for people with ID and mental health problems are being implemented all over Spain (Salvador-Carulla and Maroto 1993; Holt et al. 2000; IDRESNET 2003; Salvador-Carulla et al. 2007). Experts, health authorities, family organisations and professional associations are working together to meet the needs of this population.

For the first time, the needs of people with ID and mental health problems were included in the Catalan Mental Health Plan (2006–2010) (Departament de Salut 2006). The service model was inspired by the MHiLD model (Chaplin et al. 2008) and included a number of specialist mental health components, outpatient centres coordinated with the general mental health system as well as four sub-acute mental health hospital units in the four provinces of Catalonia. The system also incorporated community residential care and coordination with the social care sector.

In 2007, the two main organisations for the care of people with ID produced a plan to develop services for those with ID and mental health problems in Spain. This plan selected the care system in Catalonia as a benchmark and adapted it to the 17 Autonomous Regions in Spain (Salvador-Carulla et al. 2007) and it has been considered by other Autonomous Communities such as Extremadura, Castilla y Leon, Castilla La Mancha, Canary Islands, and Galicia. In the meantime, in Madrid two residential centres for sub-acute care, a day centre and a specialised outpatient community centre have opened.

AUSTRALIA

Historical context

Australia is a federation of six states, two major mainland territories and other minor territories, covering a land base of 7,686,850 km^2 with a population of 21 million. The state and territory governments are responsible for the provision of free public hospital and related community health services including mental health services. Private fee for service medical and certain other health services are subsidised by Medicare, a federal universal health insurance scheme. Private health insurance offsets the cost of private hospital stays.

Historically, institutional care of people with ID was the responsibility of state health departments. The shift from institutional to community care of people with ID split the provision of health services from social services. In general, state disability services are responsible for accommodation and occupational services while health and mental health needs are assumed by policy-makers to be met by generic health and mental health services, although the configuration and organisation of both disability and health services vary from state to state.

Generic public mental health services have failed to meet the mental health needs of Australians with ID (Parmenter 1988; Moloney 1993; Einfeld 1997). The Human Rights and Equal Opportunity Commission concluded that there was 'an urgent need for academic research, increased clinical expertise and substantial increased resources' (Burdekin 1993). The needs of people with ID and mental health problems have been acknowledged in key national policy documents over the past decade. The Second National Mental Health Plan (Australian Health Ministers 1998) identified people with ID as one of the target groups with high-level needs and called for improved treatment and care, improved access to and response by services; however, this was to be achieved using existing resources. An evaluation of the Second National Mental Health Plan (Steering Committee for the Evaluation of the Second National Mental Health Plan 1998–2003, 2003) concluded that the development and implementation of effective mental health service models for people with ID had not been realised and needed to be afforded higher priority. The National Mental Health Plan 2003–2008 (Australian Health Ministers 2003) calls for better coordination of existing services for people with complex needs but makes no mention of the need for specialist expertise or clinical services.

Services today

There are few specialist mental health services for people with ID in Australia. These are limited in scope, such as consultation-only services, or tend to be *ad hoc* initiatives of psychiatrists with an interest in ID, or are provided by academic units in developmental disability health (Centre for Developmental Disability Health Victoria (CDDHV), Monash University; Queensland Centre for Intellectual and Developmental Disability (QCIDD), University of Queensland), rather than being driven by coherent policy.

This policy failure is reflected in a series of surveys of Australian psychiatrists over the past decade (Lennox and Chaplin 1996; Edwards et al. 2007; Jess et al. 2008; Torr et al. 2008). The findings are similar across states and over time. Psychiatrists in Australia agree that adults with ID receive a poor standard of care in both in-patient and community mental health settings, that antipsychotics are over-prescribed and that a higher standard of care would be provided by specialist services if they existed. Psychiatrists are also concerned about the interface between mental health and disability services and the training and support of direct support workers.

Australian psychiatrists and trainees report that they are not well trained in the assessment and management of mental health and behaviour problems in people with ID, they tend not to make specific diagnoses and many would prefer not to work with people with ID (Lennox and Chaplin 1995; Lennox and Chaplin 1996; Edwards et al. 2007; Jess et al. 2008; Torr et al. 2008). The Royal Australian and New Zealand College of Psychiatrists has no mandatory training requirements in ID (Royal Australian and New Zealand College of Psychiatrists 2003). The development of clinical expertise is limited by the small numbers of people seen with ID and limited opportunities for specialist clinical training.

There is, though, cause for optimism that there will be improvements in specialist mental health service provision to people with ID in Australia as well as new opportunities for training. Victoria, New South Wales (NSW) and Queensland have quite different initiatives to address mental health needs of people with ID.

In Victoria, a state-wide mental health in ID service has provided consultation and training to state-run area mental health services (AMHS) over the past decade (Bennett 2000) and provides one training position for a psychiatry registrar. There are limitations to this service in that a person with ID must first access the AMHS. AMHS limits services to serious mental illness such as psychoses and high-risk mood disorders, and these disorders may not be recognised in a referred person with ID. A Victorian government green paper on mental health reform includes a section asking how mental health services for people with ID can be improved (Victorian Government Department of Human Services 2008).

In 2007 the NSW government funded the first Chair in Disability Mental Health in Australia. The position was established to increase workforce capacity to deliver appropriate and effective mental health services to people with ID as well as establishing research into mental health and ID. This will build on the existing hospital clinics operated by psychiatrists with long-term interest in ID.

Queensland has maintained a 31-bed facility for people with ID and mental disorders who require extended in-patient care and rehabilitation, which is to the author's knowledge the only specialist in-patient facility for people with ID in Australia. In 2007 the Carter Report on the plight of people with ID and violent challenging behaviour was tabled in the Queensland Parliament. In response the Queensland government has pledged substantial resources for specialist behavioural support services integrating disability and mental health services. Teams will include a range of professionals including psychologists, occupational therapists, speech and language pathologists, psychiatric nurses, neuropsychologists, psychiatrists and general practitioners. A centre of excellence will provide an academic and research base.

With the exception of South Australia, the remaining states and territories have no initiatives to address specifically the mental health needs of people with ID. South Australia has recently funded a full-time psychiatrist position in ID psychiatry, but as yet does not have a specialist mental health service for people with ID.

Over the past decade the CDDHV, Monash University and the QCIDD, University of Queensland have developed close links with MHiLD service and Estia Centre. Both centres aim to improve the health and well-being of adults with intellectual and developmental disability through the provision of clinical services, professional education and research. Collaboration with CDDHV developed online learning programmes in the psychiatry of intellectual and developmental disability for psychiatry registrars. Collaboration with QCIDD led to the development of a mental health training package for Australian support workers of those with ID (Edwards et al. 2003).

HONG KONG

Historical context

Hong Kong covers an area of about 1000 km^2 and has a current population of about 6.8 million (Census & Statistical Department 2007). The history of psychiatry in Hong Kong started in 1875 when the first asylum was opened (Lo 2003). In the subsequent 100 years, psychiatry was gradually modernised with the opening of new psychiatric facilities, training of more qualified psychiatric personnel and the development of subspecialties. The earliest sign of developing a specialised medical service for people with ID appeared in 1972 with the opening of the Siu Lam Subnormal Hospital, an institution with 300 beds that provided infirmary services to adults with severe and profound ID. Apart from this small group, all other people with ID and mental illness or behavioural disorders were covered under Hong Kong's generic mental health service.

With the promotion of the concept of normalisation (Nirje 1972; Wolfensberger 1972) and backed by the burgeoning economy of Hong Kong in the second half of the twentieth century, the Social Welfare Department and NGOs started to open community services for adults with ID. These included group homes, hostels, sheltered workshops and day activity centres. The increasing presence of people with ID, together with the input from the parents' groups, succeeded in convincing some health care managers and administrators to put more emphasis on ID services.

In 1994, the Siu Lam Outreach Service was commenced, with the primary objective of assessing the eligibility and suitability of people with ID who were applying for their infirmary service. At the same time, the team started to provide psychiatric care and support for other people in community ID facilities.

A breakthrough occurred in the following year (1995) when one of the two mental hospitals – Kwai Chung Hospital (KCH) – decided to develop a new specialist psychiatric service for adults with ID. At that time, KCH consisted of a total of 1622 psychiatric beds distributed over 34 wards and there were four psychiatric outpatient clinics located within its catchment area. Altogether, the in-patient and outpatient facilities provided mental health services for about one-quarter of the total population of Hong Kong. A hospital survey conducted in that year found that about 10% of the in-patient population were patients with ID and mental illness or behavioural disorder (Kwok 2001). It was acknowledged that specialised skills and knowledge were required to care for this population who constituted a significant proportion of those 'difficult to discharge'. Setting up a specialist team for ID was part of the process of deinstitutionalisation and was intended to help reduce the total number of in-patients of the mental hospital.

Services today

As a result, the first psychiatric unit for ID in Hong Kong was formally opened in Kwai Chung Hospital in 1996. It was headed by a specialist ID psychiatrist who had worked previously at MHiLD service and Estia Centre to acquire specialist knowledge and clinical skills for assessing and treating psychiatric problems in people with ID. The mission of this specialist unit was to meet the mental health needs of people with ID by providing a high-quality, coordinated and comprehensive psychiatric service that incorporated the principles of normalisation and community integration.

The in-patient service consists of one male and one female ward, each with 40 beds. This service is supported by multidisciplinary staff and provides an appropriate environment for specialist assessment and treatment for people whose mental health needs cannot be met in the community. Close links with families and community carers are maintained, with much emphasis on transfer of intervention skills so as to facilitate early and successful discharge of patients. Outpatient service carries an equally important weighting as the clinic is serving a catchment population of about 1.5 million. In addition, intervention may also be in the form of outreach services. By seeing patients in hostels, group homes, day centres or sheltered workshops, the team can work closely with other professional carers and family members to ensure that practical advice can be delivered directly and treatment programmes (e.g. behavioural modification) successfully implemented.

In subsequent years the unit has grown significantly, with further increases in service elements and the creation of specific programmes to meet the needs of people with ID. It has been accredited by the Royal College of Psychiatrists as a training centre on the psychiatry of ID. It has also become a model for another mental hospital (Castle Peak Hospital) to set up its own specialist service in another region of Hong Kong. The unit maintains close collaboration with the MHiLD service and Estia Centre, and continues to benefit from their support in the form of academic programmes and clinical attachments for its multidisciplinary trainees.

THE ROCHESTER MODEL (USA)

Historical context

In 1989, reports first appeared of a model community-based service to stabilise behavioural or psychiatric episodes occurring in people with ID that threatened to limit or curtail their options for remaining independent (Davidson et al. 1989, 1995; Davidson & O'Hara 2007). The model linked a tertiary specialised psychiatric in-patient unit to effect stabilisation with both specialised and generic behavioural and psychiatric clinics, to provide ongoing community-based follow-up and medium- or long-term treatment. One key feature of the model was its comprehensiveness. Another feature was that its funding was derived largely from grants, rather than fees for service. Unlike the programmes in the UK that were a part of the overall health system, the model was too costly to maintain as an integrated component of a larger mental health delivery system funded from insurance resources (Davidson et al. 1995). It was felt that components such as the community-based crisis intervention team might remain viable because of their relatively high throughput and comparatively low cost. But components that assured availability of in-patient options for initial crisis stabilisation and access to ongoing follow-up care would not be sustainable.

Between 1989 and 2000, myriad changes occurred in the array of community-based options available to people with ID. In the US, there was a nationwide effort to depopulate aggregate residential care in favour of small-group or individual community-based residential options. This systemic change was mandated by legislative and regulatory changes limiting expenditures of federal funds for aggregate care (Braddock et al. 2008). Simultaneously, health (and therefore mental health) care financing was moving from a fee-for-service based system to one that was increasingly dominated by managed care options (Birenbaum 1999). These two strategic changes created acute and persistent barriers to providing adequate services and supports to people with ID and concomitant mental health and behavioural problems. While managed care plan managers were limiting options for extended and comprehensive community-based mental health services, people with ID and mental health problems required these very services to enable them to leave aggregate care for less restrictive residential and work options in the community.

Meanwhile, the predictions referred to above came true. The Rochester model lost key components that would have prevented some of the barriers created by the conflict between managed care and full inclusion of people with ID. Grant funding of specialised in-patient mental health services ended, followed quickly by the elimination of the specialty services themselves, which could not survive the lack of funding from managed care. But enough of a residual legacy was left in place in several local tertiary in-patient units to support 'specialised' care within the generic system. ID community agencies that relied on long-term behavioural services and consultations from the crisis intervention team acted to increase their indigenous capacity to provide such services under their own comprehensive care systems. The overall cost to any one agency was minimised by the near universality across local provider agencies to establish their own response capacity. So in an unanticipated sequence of events, the system reinvented itself.

Some of these outcomes would not have occurred if the original Rochester Model had not been based in a regional university medical centre. This component of the model afforded access to both pre-service and continuing professional education programmes that, in turn, made specialised training available to health and mental health students and professionals representing key disciplines needed to staff community-based specialty programmes. Many of these trainees went on to become leaders in the local community and to exercise entrepreneurial influence on the development of new service options within the generic health, mental health and ID systems. Several collaborated on research (including colleagues at MHiLD service and Estia Centre) that led to publications in the scientific literature. There was also a shift in the training culture within the medical centre towards a positive view of the need to develop skill sets for providing services and supports to people with ID and mental health problems which sustained components of the medical school and nursing school curricula to address diagnosis and treatment services for this group. The students welcomed this, since they were aware that people with ID now lived and worked in the communities where they would be practising and that their caseloads would include people with ID and mental health problems.

Services today

The system continues to change and there are potential threats. For instance, the increase in diagnosis of autistic spectrum disorders coupled with the necessity for providing community-based services for both children of school age and adults of working age is already making demands on the service system that may be difficult to address. Secondly, the greying of the general population is mirrored in survival trends among people with ID

(Janicki et al. 1999). There are suggestions that these trends may be accompanied by shifts in mental health status (Cain et al. 2003; Davidson et al. 2003; Janicki et al. 2002; Stawski et al. 2006) but the details of the impact are not yet clear. Changes in skill set training needs, treatment modalities and shifts in residential service options will become increasingly important as these cohorts age. However, in Rochester a *bona fide* community network has been created with a sustainable future. Only unanticipated changes in funding are likely to disrupt this apparently optimistic future.

CONCLUSION

The collaboration between the MHiLD service and Estia Centre and colleagues in the UK and farther afield, as illustrated above, has had mutual benefits. Many of the issues faced in providing mental health services to people with ID have been universal, for example the move towards social care in the community resulted in a loss of mental health provision for this client group, and many mental health workers and direct care staff lacked knowledge and skills in working with those with ID and mental health problems. The efforts, often of a few key people, supported by the voices of clients and their families enabled a sharing of skills and experience through consultation, visits, teaching activities, research and clinical initiatives.

People with ID, especially those with mental health problems, tend to be marginalised. Such collaborations, sometimes informal and at other times formalised through organisations such as the European Association for People with Mental Health Problem and ID and the ID Section of the World Psychiatric Association, support clinicians and others to advocate for this client group's need for appropriate services.

Several countries around the world are trying to address the mental health needs of their population with ID. Unfortunately there is a paucity of information from the developing world. Currently efforts are being made to encourage similar developments by promoting professional collaborations and supporting relevant publications (Jeevanandam 2009; Njenga 2009; Mercadante and Paula 2009 in press).

NECESSARY STEPS TO BETTER SERVICES

There is an International consensus from the existing data that mental health services for people with ID and mental health problems should include:

- some form of service specialisation
- community outreach and in-patient facilities
- strong links with both general mental health and ID services

- provision by the health service
- collaboration between health and social care sectors
- specialist training.

REFERENCES

Australian Health Ministers (1998) *Second National Mental Health Plan*. Canberra: Mental Health Branch, Commonwealth Department of Health and Family Services.

Australian Health Ministers (2003) *National Mental Health Plan 2003–2008*. Canberra: Australian Government.

Bennett, C. (2000) The Victorian Dual Disability Service. *Australasian Psychiatry*, 8 (3), 238–242.

Bigby, C. and Ozanne, E. (2001) Shifts in the model of service delivery in intellectual disability in Victoria. *Journal of Intellectual and Developmental Disability*, 26 (2), 177–190.

Birenbaum, A. (1999) *Disability and Managed Care: Problems and Opportunities at the End of the Century*. Westport, CT: Praeger.

Bouras, N. (ed.) (1994) *Mental Health in Mental Retardation: Recent Advances and Practices*. Cambridge, UK: Cambridge University Press.

Bouras, N. and Holt, G. (2001) Psychiatric treatment and community care. In A. Dosen and K. Day (eds), *Treating Mental Illness and Behavior Disorders in Children and Adults with Mental Retardation* (pp. 493–502). Washington, DC: American Psychiatric Press.

Bouras, N., Kon, Y. and Drummond, C. (1993) Medical and psychiatric needs of adults with a mental handicap. *Journal of Intellectual Disability Research*, 37, 177–182.

Braddock, D., Hemp, R. and Rizzolo, M.C. (2008) *The State of the States in Developmental Disabilities*. Washington, DC: American Association on Intellectual and Developmental Disabilities.

Burdekin, B. (1993) *Report of the National Inquiry into the Human Rights of People with Mental Illness*. Canberra: Australian Government Publishing Service.

Cain, N.N., Davidson, P.W., Burhan, A.M., Andolsek, M.E., Baxter, J.T., Sullivan, L., Florescure, H., List, A. and Deutsch, L. (2003) Identifying bipolar disorders in individuals with intellectual disability. *Journal of Intellectual Disability Research*, 47, 31–38.

Census & Statistics Department (2007) *Hong Kong Population Projections 2007–2036*. Hong Kong: SAR Government.

Chaplin, E., O'Hara, J., Holt, G,. Hardy, S. and Bouras, N. (2008) MHiLD: A model of specialist mental health services for people with learning disabilities. *Advances in Mental Health and Learning Disabilities*, 2 (4), 46–50.

Davidson, P.W., Peloquin, L.J., Salzman, L., Zeilinski, S., Gross, M. and Roberts, K. (1989) Planning and implementing comprehensive crisis intervention for people with developmental disabilities. In J. Levy, P. Levy, and B. Niven (eds), *Strengthening Families: New Directions in Providing Services to People with Developmental Disabilities and Their Families*. New York: Young Adult Institute Press.

Davidson, P.W., Cain, N., Sloane-Reeves, J., Giesow, V., Quijano, L., VanHeyningen, J. and Shoham, I. (1995) Crisis intervention for community-based persons with developmental disabilities and concomitant behavioral and psychiatric disorders. *Mental Retardation*, 33 (1), 21–30.

Davidson, P.W., Janicki, M.P., Ladrigan, P., Houser, K., Henderson, C.M. and Cain, N.C. (2003) Association between behavior problems and health status in older adults with intellectual ability. *Ageing and Mental Health*, 7 (6), 424–430.

Davidson, P.W. and O'Hara, J. (2007) Clinical services for people with intellectual disabilities and psychiatric or severe behaviour disorders. In N. Bouras and G. Holt (eds), *Psychiatric and Behavioural Disorders in Intellectual and Developmental Disabilities* (2nd ed., pp. 364–387). Cambridge, UK: Cambridge University Press.

Departament de Salut (2006) *Direcció General de Planificació i Avaluació. Pla Director de Salut Mental i Adiccions.* Barcelona: Generalitat de Catalunya.

Department of Health and Children (2006) *A Vision for Change.* Dublin, Ireland: Government Publications Office.

Dosen, A. (2005) *Psychische stoornissen, gedragsproblemen en verstandelijke handicap.* Assen, The Netherlands: Van Gorcum.

Edwards, N., Lennox, N., Holt, G. and Bouras, N. (eds) (2003) *Mental Health in Adult Development Disability: The Dual Diagnosis Education and Training Kit.* Brisbane, Australia: University of Queensland.

Edwards, N., Lennox, N. and White, P. (2007) Queensland psychiatrists' attitudes and perceptions of adults with intellectual disability. *Journal of Intellectual Disability Research,* 51 (1), 75–81.

Einfeld, S. (1997) Intellectual handicap in contemporary psychiatry. *Australian and New Zealand Journal of Psychiatry,* 31, 452–456.

Holt, G., Costello, H., Bouras, N., Diareme, S., Hillery, J., Moss, S., Rodriguez-Blaquez, C., Salvador, L., Tsiantis, J., Weber, G. and Dimitrakaki, C. (2000) BIOMED-MEROPE Project: Service provision for adults with mental retardation: A European comparison. *Journal of Intellectual Disability Research,* 44, 685–696.

IDRESNET (European Intellectual Disability Research Network) (2003) *Intellectual Disability in Europe: Working Papers.* Canterbury, UK: Tizard Centre, University of Kent at Canterbury.

Janicki, M.P., Dalton, A.R., Henderson, C.M. and Davidson, P.W. (1999) Mortality and morbidity among older adults with intellectual disabilities: Health services considerations. *Disability and Rehabilitation,* 21 (5–6), 284–294.

Janicki, M.P., Davidson, P.W., Henderson, C.M., McCallion, P., Taets, J.D., Force, L.T., Sulkes, S.B., Frangenberg, E. and Ladrigan, P.M. (2002) Health characteristics and health services utilization in older adults with intellectual disabilities living in community residences. *Journal of Intellectual Disability Research,* 46, 287–298.

Jeevanandam, L. (2009) Perspectives of intellectual disability in Asia: Epidemiology, policy, and services for children and adults. *Current Opinion in Psychiatry,* 22 (5), 462–468.

Jess, G., Torr, J., Cooper, S.-A., Lennox, N.G., Edwards, N., Galea, J. and O'Brien, G. (2008) Specialist versus generic models of psychiatry training and service provision for people with intellectual disabilities. *Journal of Applied Research in Intellectual Disabilities,* 21, 183–193.

Kennedy, J.F. (1961) Statement by the President regarding the need for a national plan in mental retardation, October 11, 1961. In *The National Action to Combat Mental Retardation.* Washington, DC: The President's Panel on Mental Retardation, October 1962.

Kwok, H. (2001) The development of a specialized psychiatric service for people with learning disabilities and mental health problems: Report of a project from Kwai Chung Hospital Hong Kong. *British Journal of Learning Disabilities,* 29, 22–25.

Kwok, H. and Chui, E. (2008) A survey on mental health care for adults with intellectual disabilities in Asia. *Journal of Intellectual Disability Research,* 52, 996–1002.

Lennox, N. and Chaplin, R. (1995) The psychiatric care of people with intellectual disabilities: The perceptions of trainee psychiatrists and psychiatric medical officers. *Australian & New Zealand Journal of Psychiatry,* 29 (4), 632–637.

Lennox, N. and Chaplin, R. (1996) The psychiatric care of people with intellectual disabilities: The perceptions of consultant psychiatrists in Victoria. *Australian and New Zealand Journal of Psychiatry,* 30, 774–780.

Lo, W.H. (2003) A century (1885 to 1985) of development of psychiatric services in Hong

Kong – with special reference to personal experience. *Hong Kong Journal of Psychiatry*, 13, 21–29.

Mercadante, M.T., Evans-Lacko, S. and Paula, C.S. (2009) Perspectives of intellectual disability in Latin America countries: Epidemiology, policy, and services for children and adults. *Current Opinion in Psychiatry*, 22 (5), 469–474.

Moloney, H. (1993) Mental health services for people with intellectual disability: Current developments. *Australian and New Zealand Journal of Developmental Disabilities*, 18, 169–176.

Nirje, B. (1972) The right to self-determination. In W. Wolfensberger (ed.), *The Principle of Normalization in Human Services*. Toronto, Canada: National Institute on Mental Retardation.

Njenga, F. (2009) Perspectives of intellectual disability in Africa: Epidemiology and policy services for children and adults. *Current Opinion in Psychiatry*, 22 (5), 457–461.

Parmenter, T. (1988) An analysis of Australian mental health services for people with mental retardation. *Australian and New Zealand Journal of Developmental Disabilities*, 14, 9–14.

President's Committee for People with Intellectual Disabilities (2004) *Report to the President: A Charge We Have to Keep: A Road Map to Personal and Economic Freedom for Persons with Intellectual Disabilities*. Washington, DC: PCPID.

Royal Australian & New Zealand College of Psychiatrists (2003) *RANZCP Training and Assessment Regulations 2003*. Melbourne, Australia: RANZCP.

Royal College of Psychiatrists (2004) *Occasional Paper 58: A Proposed Model for the Delivery of a Mental Health Service to People with Intellectual Disability*. London: RCP.

Salvador-Carulla, L., Martínez-Leal, R., Salinas, J.A. (2007) Análisis del impacto de plan estratégico sobre atención a los trastornos mentales y problemas del comportamiento en las personas con discapacidad intelectual. En: *Trastornos de la salud mental en las personas con discapacidad intelectual*. Madrid, Spain: FEAPS.

Salvador-Carulla, L. and Martínez-Maroto, A. (1993) Description of general services for people with mental handicap in Spain. *Journal of Intellectual Disability Research*, 37 (Suppl. 1), 34–37.

Stawksi, M., Davidson, P.W. and Merrick, J. (2006) Editorial: Mental health and intellectual disability. *Israel Journal of Psychiatry and Related Sciences*, 43 (4), 235–236.

Steering Committee for the Evaluation of the Second National Mental Health Plan 1998–2003 (2003) *Evaluation of the Second National Mental Health Plan*. Canberra: Commonwealth of Australia.

Torr, J., Lennox, N., Cooper, S.A., Rey-Conde, T., Ware, R.S., Galea, J. and Taylor, M. (2008) Psychiatric care of adults with intellectual disabilities: Changing perceptions over a decade. *Australian and New Zealand Journal of Psychiatry*, 42, 890–897.

Victorian Government Department of Human Services (2008) *Because mental health matters: A new focus for mental health and wellbeing in Victoria*. Consultation paper, Melbourne, Australia: May 2008.

Wolfensberger, W. (1972) *The Principle of Normalization in Human Services*. Toronto, Canada: National Institute on Mental Retardation.

PART II

Clinical practice

CHAPTER FOUR

Assessment, diagnosis and rating instruments

Andrew Flynn and Shaun Gravestock

INTRODUCTION

Among the controversies that concern clinicians working with adults with intellectual disability (ID), perhaps two in particular stand out as special challenges.

The first lies with the now historic separation of ID from mental illness, establishing the concept of 'dual diagnosis' (Reiss 1990) and, by implication, a duality of service provision for those in need: on the one hand rest the educational and social vulnerabilities that constitute the disability itself (as opposed to the impairment) and on the other the multifaceted emotional and behavioural consequences of ID that, in some individuals and under some circumstances, appear to constitute an additional and, crucially, separable mental disorder. The question arises: if such a distinction can be established in principle, to what extent can it be reliably discerned in practice (Sturmey 1999)?

The second challenge arrives on the heels of the first: if someone with ID does indeed have a nameable mental disorder, in what way is it different to the same mental disorder in the general population? To what extent is it special? To what extent is it *specialist*? Indeed, to what extent does it require the attentions of a specialist as opposed to a 'mainstream' mental health service (Gravestock 1999)?

It is against this conceptual and ideological backdrop that the assessment and diagnosis of mental disorder in people with ID needs to be considered. How these questions are approached has deep implications for the mental health practitioner, the commissioner of services and the academic researcher, not to mention, of course, the individual faced with the prospect of moving from client-with-problem to patient-with-illness.

In this chapter we will consider some of the key issues that make the assessment of mental health problems in ID arguably a specialist business and, as mental health practice increasingly aspires to becoming the practice of mental health science, the ways in which the measurement of psychiatric symptoms and syndromes in this group of people has evolved.

SPECIAL ISSUES IN ASSESSMENT

The traditional psychiatric assessment follows many lines of personal and social enquiry and is expected to achieve many ends. However, one of the most important of these – arguably the most important – is to identify the states of mind that underlie, and may even be considered to cause, expressions of emotional distress or behavioural disturbance, i.e. the mental state. The avoidance of dogs (a behaviour), say, occurring in a state of distress (from which the emotion of anxiety might be inferred) accompanied by seemingly exaggerated worries about the dangerousness of dogs in general (the distorted cognitive content of the anxious state), possibly arising from memories of being attacked by a dog in the past (a traumatic recollection): these are the links in a chain that connects past experience, current state of mind and subsequent action that history taking and examination attempt to find. Although diagnosis and treatment are the ultimate aims, at the very least both doctor and patient will hope to arrive at some sort of plausible understanding of a problem even if the way forward is not always either easy or obvious.

These things are, of course, frequently as much matters of opinion as of fact. Although any medical assessment can appear to be the collection of objective facts about events, symptoms and signs, in reality a high degree of inference is involved in all of these things (Fulford 1994). This is particularly the case in psychiatric assessment, where there is little in the way of physical signs and fewer physical investigations to support or verify personal accounts of symptoms, and even more so in the case of adults with ID, where the ability to formulate and express even these sorts of subjective account is often at issue (Cooper et al. 2003). Because surmounting this hurdle is so fundamental to psychiatric practice and research in this group of people, it is worth considering in a little more detail.

It is useful to consider the main difficulties in assessment under the following broad headings, any or all of which may be relevant in an individual case (Bouras and Hardy 2002) and all of which require special attention and, to some degree, modification of the 'conventional' approach (Prosser and Bromley 1998):

1. receptive and expressive communication problems
2. acquiescence and suggestibility
3. concept formation.

RECEPTIVE AND EXPRESSIVE COMMUNICATION IMPAIRMENTS

Difficulties with communication in all its forms are, aside from the limitations of cognitive processing *per se*, among the most characteristic and marked challenges facing people with ID (Brewster 2004). Not only are communication problems an issue for assessment and diagnosis but they are also widely implicated in the genesis and maintenance of mental health problems in themselves. Indeed, the range of clinical interventions for challenging behaviour that come under the heading of 'functional analysis' take as one of their starting points the idea that maladaptive or problem behaviour is a way of expressing a psychological or physical need that a person cannot communicate in more adaptive ways (Sturmey 1999).

The ability of people with ID to communicate effectively can be hampered for a variety of reasons, affecting both the comprehension of what is said or conveyed by others and the ability to respond effectively. So-called 'expressive' problems may arise because of limitations in vocabulary and difficulties in articulation due, for example, to large tongue size in people with Down Syndrome. In contrast, 'receptive' problems arise for reasons ranging from the ability to understand complex or unusual words or sentence constructions, to sensory impairment (for example, up to 10% of people with mild ID have hearing problems), deficits in working memory (long phrases cannot be effectively held in mind so that a response can be composed) and problems with maintaining attention or focus (Deb et al. 2001).

It is not unusual for individuals with milder degrees of ID to give an impression of competence in communication that exceeds their true abilities because of mismatches between their expressive and understanding abilities. The style of speech may be chatty and may even have a superficial sophistication; its fragility is revealed only when the person is asked to explain or expand on points in more detail. In many cases this style of verbal communication can be seen as an aid to 'passing' as normal by someone who is aware of their ID and who is striving to 'fit in' with a more able peer group or to enhance their self-image by minimising their disability. Similar mismatches can also sometimes be found with reading, where the person with ID is able to read a passage of text out loud but has little comprehension of its content. Although it can have an adaptive function, it can also lead to major problems for the person who becomes exposed to expectations that they struggle to live up to, and to the clinician who may underestimate the level of ID (Mactavish et al. 2000).

ACQUIESCENCE AND SUGGESTIBILITY

Acquiescence and suggestibility are related but distinct ideas and have been the focus of much attention in the context of the conduct of police interviews, again principally with people with milder degrees of ID. However, both, and particularly acquiescence, also occur as issues in clinical assessment.

Acquiescence is closely related to the concept of 'response bias' in the development of rating scales. This is the tendency to answer in the affirmative to closed 'yes' or 'no' questions and is known to be correlated to some extent with IQ level (Sigelman et al. 1982). Acquiescent responses are typically revealed when the same 'yes' answer is given to clearly contradictory prompts (Prosser and Bromley 1998), for example the person indicating that they feel either sad or happy in answer to consecutive questions about opposite moods: 'do you feel sad?' and 'do you feel happy?'.

In contrast, suggestibility is a more complex phenomenon and has been defined by Gudjonsson and Clare (1986) as having at least two components. The first concerns the extent to which a person can be induced to change a story they have given as a result of a negative response by the interviewer. The second is the tendency to take on alternative suggestions for details in an account as a result of leading questions and positive responses by the interviewer such that the person comes to believe the modified or suggested account. This phenomenon has been dramatically and controversially demonstrated by Elizabeth Loftus in adults without ID using her now famous 'Lost in the Mall' paradigm (see Slater 2004 for an especially absorbing review) of implanting false memories. Indeed, Loftus' research underlines the more general point that the phenomenon of suggestibility is not confined to people with ID and that factors other than intellectual impairment may constitute more important risks for its development. However, the fact remains that many of these other, psychosocial, factors crop up more often in certain vulnerable groups, adults with ID constituting one such group.

Both acquiescence and suggestibility are more likely to occur under circumstances where an interviewee feels it necessary to give answers that will please or impress the interviewer, either through a desire to gain the interviewer's esteem or because the interviewer is in some way perceived as intimidating. Alternatively, the person may be motivated by a desire to cover up gaps in knowledge (perhaps wishing not to appear 'stupid') or to fill in gaps in episodic memory (confabulation) or to try to bring an aversive experience to an end. However, it is not only the dynamics of role imbalance between patient and professional and problems arising directly from cognitive impairment that may give rise to induced, erroneous accounts: factors such as tiredness, hunger, pain, and emotional distress are also important (Mactavish et al. 2000).

CONCEPT FORMATION

Assessment interviews are often complicated by the degree to which the person with ID has developed a reliable appreciation of certain key concepts. Locating events in time is possibly the most frequently encountered in clinical practice, but knowledge of the basic internal workings of the body (organ concept) and a system for identifying, labelling and quantifying personal emotional states is often only sketchily formed. For example, subject-based diagnostic assessment of the DC-LD eating disorders was not possible in most adults with severe ID due to their limited communication skills and limited weight, body shape and size conceptualisation skills. This was despite trying to use supporting androgynous body shapes as pictorial prompts to assess perceived and ideal body image (Gravestock 2003; Gravestock and McCluskey 2009).

Although categories for events, objects, personal attributes, relationships and mental states may be absent or only partially formed, they may also become over-extended (e.g. the word 'depression' being used to describe all dysphoric mood states) or overly restricted (as occurs in concrete thinking, for example in autistic spectrum disorder) compared with their conventional use (Flynn 2008).

THE CLINICAL INTERVIEW

These considerations play a major part in how the traditional psychiatric interview is modified when working with people with ID (Bouras and Hardy 2002; Prosser and Bromley 1998). Special emphasis is placed, for instance, on obtaining background information prior to interview where possible, and involving a key informant in the interview process both to support the person and to corroborate or provide information (Deb et al. 2001). Interviews may need to be shorter on occasion than the traditional 'psychiatric hour', with assessment extended over several meetings.

In the interview itself, sentences are shortened and simplified so that they contain single clauses and single ideas; questions are phrased in the active (e.g. *did you make the tea?*) rather than the passive (*was the tea made by you?*) voice; jargon is avoided and everyday words preferred; special care is taken over the use of figurative speech (*what do you do for a living?* in contrast to *what job do you do?*); special care is taken over the use of metaphor and colloquialism, both of which are very prone to being mis-understood, particularly by individuals with a literal style of interpretation; abstract and speculative questions are reframed to be more concrete and based in the present or recent past; and questions involving time concepts make special use of anchor events, well-defined and personally meaningful temporal points such as Christmas about which other events can be organised. Throughout the interview checks on understanding are made, content is regularly summarised back, open-ended questions to introduce avenues of enquiry are carefully balanced against more closed questions with consequent attention to acquiescent responding, and, possibly most challenging even for the experienced interviewer, the movement of ques-tioning between informant and patient is carefully managed so that the person with ID does not become neglected or isolated within the assess-ment, or, worse still, talked about in the third person (Mactavish et al. 2000; Brewster 2004).

SOME CONSIDERATIONS IN THE DEVELOPMENT OF PSYCHOPATHOLOGICAL RATING SCALES FOR PEOPLE WITH ID

Throughout the twentieth century psychiatry worked hard to justify itself as a branch of medicine with a scientific foundation, to prove that it deals in phenomena that: can be objectively and unambiguously defined; can be categorised within a natural system whose joints are, at least in principle, carveable; can be reliably measured; are ultimately located in the physical (as opposed to metaphysical) world; and are amenable to broadly conceived medical interventions. The standardised rating instrument has been central to these efforts.

The history of rating instruments for people with ID and coexisting mental health problems has followed three distinct pathways: the adapta-tion of existing instruments normally used in the non-ID population; the unmodified (or minimally modified) use of existing instruments again intended for the non-ID population; and the construction of new instru-ments for specific use with people with ID. Instruments can be further classified according to their focus of interest. Some, for example, restrict themselves to the diagnosis of disorder, others the general quantification of symptoms, the quantification of specific symptoms of particular disorders or the measurement of aspects of mental disorder (adaptive function, need) that are separable from the symptoms themselves but play an important part in treatment planning and monitoring of overall benefit. Finally, instruments can be divided into those that rely on self-report, third-party account, direct observation or structured or semi-structured interview (Sturmey et al. 1991; Sturmey 1999).

In a review that was comprehensive at the time, Sturmey and colleagues (1991) identified eight 'emerging issues' that they felt needed to be resolved as research on psychopathology in people with ID progressed and, it was hoped, matured. Among these were their observations that modifications of instruments developed for use in the general population were rarely if ever subjected to subsequent re-evaluation either by comparing their parallel form properties with the original or checking that the modifications (whether to item content or the format of the test) improved response rates or tallied better with clinical impression. Indeed, problems with establishing clear gold-standards for diagnosis or disorder severity against which the performance of instruments could be judged were at the heart of another three of their eight concerns. Proper validation, clear consensus for diagnosis (particularly for schizophrenia) and 'careful consideration of how systems of classification, such as DSM-III-R and ICD-10-D criteria can be applied to people with learning [intellectual] difficulties' were their principal recommendations, with the implication that without attention to such matters the marked growth in research that had begun in the 1980s might produce findings would always be open to substantial question or be of dubious value in the clinic (Cooper et al. 2003; Bouras 2004).

In much the same way that Binet's early tests of intellectual capabilities inspired the development of the various measures of IQ available today (either as direct descendants or as reactions in one way or another to their shortcomings), the progenitor for many of the currently available rating and assessment instruments is probably the Psychopathology Instrument for Mentally Retarded Adults (PIMRA; Matson et al. 1984). A method for assessing psychopathology across a broad range of clinical presentations, the PIMRA's primary aim was to measure and classify emotional and behavioural presentations according to the framework of DSM-III to help, among other things, with mental health insurance payments in the US (Senatore et al. 1985). The seven subscales included psychiatric standards such as schizophrenic disorder and affective disorders as well as the more obscure inappropriate mental adjustment. Although the developers of the PIMRA reported it to have reasonably robust psychometric characteristics, subsequent investigators found that it had poorer (and in the case of two of its subscales much poorer) internal consistencies than originally supposed (Sturmey and Ley 1990). Other independent studies showed that its factor structure in fact mapped rather poorly onto the DSM categories it was intended to correspond to (Aman et al. 1986) and that the correlation between the informant and self-report versions of the PIMRA that had been developed was unimpressive (Watson et al. 1988). Watson et al. went on to question the whole enterprise of trying to develop psychopathology measures for people with ID based on DSM; or at least, we might presume, DSM in its unmodified form.

It is notable that the PIMRA has almost dropped from sight in psychiatric research. However, to date it remains probably the most extensively researched psychopathological rating instrument in people with ID and it is rare for it to go uncited in the studies of other scales that have appeared since.

Aside from questions of the appropriateness of using unmodified diagnostic categories for people with ID (Cooper et al. 2003), some of the controversies stoked by the PIMRA concerned the best way of getting accurate and reliable insight into the mental state of the person with ID and coexistent mental health problems (Deb et al. 2001). Although the same conundrum exists in the general population, it has always stood out in this group for reasons previously discussed. Bramston and Fogarty (2000) compared three methods – rating by a key informant, self-report and clinical interview – as ways of assessing emotional disorder in people with mild and moderate degrees of ID. Because of the problems in controlling for levels of literacy, the self-report measures (including Spielberger's State-Trait Anger Expression Inventory and Kovacs's Children's Depression Inventory, the latter a recognised descendant of the Beck Depression Inventory (BDI)) were administered in an interview format with appropriate minor rewording as necessary so that statements (e.g. 'I am quick tempered') were converted into questions ('Are you quick tempered?'). Additional checks on understanding were made and the interviewer was permitted to clarify (and, it must be supposed, interpret) as necessary. Finally, pictorial supports were also available to help understanding. The clinical and informant assessments were designed to resemble usual clinical practice with ratings made on a five-point Likert scale. Although the investigators found a modest degree of convergence between self-report and clinical interview overall (perhaps not surprising given the way in which the self-reports were administered), the degree of overlap between the different methods was low.

The question arises as to whose account of psychopathology is the most correct in any individual's case (Moss et al. 1996a) or, as in the old story of the three blind men fumbling around the elephant, what are the particular merits of varied perspectives? In clinical work balanced judgements based on multiple sources of information are made after, in some cases, much deliberation and even revision, and uncertainty is never entirely dissipated. However, for the purpose of research where it may be necessary to reach rather more concrete conclusions in large groups of people in a relatively short space of time, trade-offs must inevitably be made between validity, practicality and clinical utility. For this reason, a considerable degree of effort continues to be invested in abbreviated assessment and self-report formats (Deb et al. 2001).

Bramston and Fogarty's study highlights an important limitation with generic self-report measures for people with ID and the necessity of modifying aspects of the content or method of delivery if people with ID are to have any reasonable hope of making use of them beyond making educated guesses in a multiple-choice quiz. But once a test is changed even by a little it can no longer be assumed to retain the properties it formerly had even in the population for which it was conceived in the first place, let alone a different one. Specifics of the methodological issues of either modifying scales for people with ID or developing them from scratch are reviewed in detail by Finlay and Lyons (2001): not surprisingly, they bear more than a passing resemblance to the principles underlying Prosser and Bromley's advice on clinical interviewing.

But how much modification is needed? Powell (2003) investigated the psychometric properties of two well-known and widely used self-report measures of severity of depressive illness in the general population in adults with ID who had been screened with a brief pre-test (and hence would almost certainly be individuals with milder ID) as being able to comprehend and complete the format but not on the basis of prior psychiatric diagnosis. With only a basic level of investigator support – confined to explaining the meanings of difficult words, reading items out loud and supplementing the Zung's semantic differential scale with a bar-graph alternative – the two scales produced a significant correlation with one another. Importantly, while the BDI's factor structure for the adults with ID mirrored that in the wider population, the Zung's shortcomings in this group (low internal consistency and unstable factor structure) mirrored those in the non-ID population.

This is encouraging in itself but even such a well-known instrument as the BDI – one that was already widely used in clinical practice in ID because of its perceived usefulness – still falls short of the eight standards set by Sturmey et al. (1991), in particular the failure to establish a standard for diagnosing depression in the first place (the BDI is, of course, not intended to be diagnostic and its proper use is confined to those already clinically diagnosed with depression) and also what might be regarded as an acid test – can it reliably track change in response to treatment? To date, this is not known with any certainty and therapeutic clinical trials that have successfully demonstrated treatment effects (or, in the case of the recent NACHBID trial (Tyrer et al. 2008) a *failure* of a commonly-used treatment) have relied on measures of behavioural disturbance rather than psychopathology to do so. Reliability means little in the absence of validity, which itself comes in a variety of flavours, all of which require their own attention (Moss et al. 1998; Sturmey et al. 2005).

The diagnosis of personality disorder (PD), sitting as it does in the fringes of mental health work in ID as in general settings, may ironically be one of a small number of examples where a relatively simple assessment procedure (the Standardised Assessment of Personality, SAP; Pilgrim et al.

1990), designed for use in patients without ID but with a good degree of psychometric respectability (Ballinger and Reid 1987) may have the sort of external validity that is sought for other instruments. The SAP is a brief structured interview with a key informant designed to produce ICD-10 PD diagnoses primarily for epidemiological research; it makes no use of observation or reports by patients themselves, a feature that sparked initial interest in its use as a way of bypassing communication difficulties. In a study of in-patients with mild to moderate ID (Flynn et al. 2002) it was shown that not only could research diagnoses tally (albeit imperfectly) with clinical ones, and so had face validity, but they also correlated strongly with experiences of childhood abuse and neglect, long established as central risk factors for similar diagnoses in general psychiatric patients. The national practice (NICE) guidelines in the UK for the management of borderline and antisocial PD, both of which include people with ID who have these conditions, may provide for the SAP to become an important and simple tool in clinical practice.

We describe below the three recent and potentially important instruments that were designed specifically for use with adults with ID, each taking as its focus of interest a different aspect of mental health.

HEALTH OF THE NATION OUTCOME SCALE FOR LEARNING DISABILITY (HONOS-LD)

Following the publication of the UK government's Health of the Nation targets for mental health in the mid-1990s, instruments were produced for a variety of specialist areas of mental health practice as a way for them to monitor (and ultimately demonstrate) relevant change in clinical status for individual patients and were intended to be easy for busy clinicians to incorporate into day-to-day practice.

The version of HoNOS designed for adults with ID is a broad assessment, covering 18 present state areas ranging from aspects of behavioural disturbance (three items in total), cognitive and communicative function (four items) and psychotic and affective symptoms (one item each) to physical health (two items, one being epilepsy), functional level (four items, including one for occupation) and state of relationships (assessed on a single item). Sleep and appetite are also rated separately from problems in other areas. Despite its apparent simplicity, the scales have potentially complex relationships with one another (e.g. behavioural disturbance is used as a guide to establishing severity on the psychosis scale but may also be separately coded in the aggression to others or self-injury domains regardless of its connection with a psychotic process) although details of its psychometric properties and factor structure remain unpublished.

HoNOS-LD in several ways stands out as probably the most ambitious of the rating scales developed for assessing mental health problems in people with ID. It is brief, designed with all levels of ID in mind, intended to be completed following routine clinical encounters following a basic training and to cover not only the symptoms of mental illness but also aspects of its consequences, complications and comorbidities. It is not, however, a diagnostic instrument and does not set out to quantify need.

The initial field trial of HoNOS-LD (Roy et al. 2002) reported good inter-rater reliability across two points in time and substantial correlation with ratings on the Aberrant Behaviour Checklist (Aman and Singh 1985), a long-established measure of behavioural disturbance. In addition, there were indications that the instrument would indeed be able to detect the sort of clinical change that would truly establish its value in clinical as well as research practice. However, the data to support this was less strong and it is a question that remains to be definitively settled, especially in relation to the often chronic, multiple and complex mental health needs of adults with intellectual disability (Pickard and Gravestock 2001). Perhaps because of this the HoNOS-LD has not received much subsequent attention in the literature and no studies using it as therapeutic outcome measure have so far appeared.

THE PSYCHIATRIC ASSESSMENT SCHEDULE FOR ADULTS WITH DEVELOPMENTAL DISABILITY (PAS-ADD)

PAS-ADD (Moss et al. 1993) is a semi-structured interviewer-rated instrument intended to produce psychiatric diagnoses in terms of ICD-10 research criteria with historical links to Wing's Present State Examination (PSE), and is a direct descendant of the PSE's subsequent WHO derivative, the Schedule for Clinical Assessment in Neuropsychiatry (SCAN). Multiple items are used to examine diagnostically pivotal recent psychiatric symptoms in an interview with the person with ID and a key informant (either or both of which can be incorporated into the analysis), which can then be entered into an algorithm to generate a range of diagnoses but especially schizophrenia and related disorders. Like the PSE, the PAS-ADD is designed to be conducted by experienced interviewers with additional (and substantial) training in the format itself.

One of the PAS-ADD's most important features is the attention it pays to modifying conventional diagnostic questions to meet the constraints of examining for complex and abstract mental phenomena in people with substantial cognitive and communicative difficulty, with individual items broken down into the sorts of smaller and simpler components recommended by Prosser and Bromley for routine clinical assessments. In studies by the developers of inter-rater reliabilites, kappa values of 0.65 for individual items and 0.7 for the 'caseness' of symptoms were shown. However, a subsequent study of its validity (Moss et al. 1996a) again highlighted the problems of using conventional diagnostic criteria (for example, Schneiderian first-rank symptoms) as the basis for assigning diagnoses, with clinicians identifying a significant number of individuals with schizophrenia in the sample who were not diagnosed as such by the PAS-ADD, and, conversely, the instrument assigning diagnoses of schizophrenia where clinicians opted for alternatives. Although there was still substantial concordance between clinical and PAS-ADD diagnosis, the discrepancies for schizophrenia (amounting to approximately one-third of cases) were hardly negligible. While some of the difference could likely be accounted for by the operation of the PAS-ADD itself (e.g. its concentration on current and recent symptoms only), the developers highlighted the problem of developing valid as opposed to reliable assessment tools where important aspects of the thing being measured were themselves the subject of uncertainty and where, in the absence of 'gold standards', an understanding of the rules of thumb by which practising clinicians made diagnoses in people remain opaque. Furthermore, this same study again showed just how hard it is for people with ID to identify in themselves (or to endorse) certain types of complex mental health symptom such as passivity or thought alienation in contrast to the relatively more straightforward auditory hallucination.

The PAS-ADD is a thorough though time-consuming tool and has spawned a small family of related measures, the shorter mini-PAS-ADD and, more recently, a screening instrument, the PAS-ADD Checklist (Moss et al. 1998; Sturmey et al. 2005). The Checklist appears to be moderately effective as a screening tool with respect to the likelihood of receiving a diagnosis of a mental illness in a formal subsequent clinical assessment (sensitivity 66%, specificity 70%). Whether the individuals it identifies or misses have significant levels of specialist mental health *need* (as distinct from potentially qualifying for a psychiatric diagnosis) is not known, however.

THE CAMBERWELL ASSESSMENT OF NEED FOR ADULTS WITH DEVELOPMENTAL AND INTELLECTUAL DISABILITIES (CANDID)

It is unusual for the clinical problems referred to secondary level health care services to present in isolation, and many of the challenges in treating mental illness arise because of other social and health problems that may in one way or another contribute to the onset of mental illness, complicate its treatment or confound its resolution. For these reasons, meeting aspects of need separate to those inherent in a mental illness itself may become as important as deciding on the correct dose of medication or modality of psychotherapy. Adults with ID in specialist services frequently contend not only with problems of poor housing, substance misuse or navigating the benefits system but also with problems arising more directly from facets of the ID, such as those connected with basic education or the ability to manage the sorts of personal affairs many would take for granted (Gravestock 1999).

The CANDID (Xenitidis et al. 2000) is derived from a parent instrument, the Camberwell Assessment of Need, and, in contrast to existing tools that assess the impact of disability or functional capabilities in adults with ID, was designed to be brief, relevant to people with co-occurring mental health problems and deliverable by a variety of professionals with minimal additional training. The CANDID assesses 25 areas of possible need from the perspectives of the service user and, where applicable, their carer or support staff, summing the scores to produce a single total need-score that takes account of 'met' and 'unmet' need.

The developers have shown high inter-rater reliability correlations and substantial stability of scores over time as well as significant correlation with two other measures of function, the Disability Assessment Schedule (DAS; Holmes et al. 1982; intended for ID) and the Global Assessment of Function (GAF; a 'generic' measure and the basis for Axis IV in DSM-IV). However, so far there have been no studies of its predictive validity, clinical or service utility (despite its simplicity) or of the 'equivalence' of similar total scores derived from different patterns of need in the nine years since its publication. Indeed, and despite its innovative features, it has not been made entirely clear why one might prefer it to the instruments against which it was compared – the DAS and GAF – to establish its concurrent validity.

CONCLUSION

An obvious question is what are we measuring and why? Fairly or not, psychiatry has always laboured as a Cinderella of clinical and academic medicine. More than any other medical speciality, it has found itself caught between a rock and a hard place: on one hand seeking to maintain its humanistic face, grappling with the uncertainties and ambiguities of subjective lives as lived by people while on the other showing that the phenomena it studies are real and quantifiable and that things such as minds are as scientifically amenable as the workings of any of the bodily organs, and that its illnesses are, consequently, real illnesses and as deserving as any other. It is a difficult juggling act, neatly encapsulated by the image many psychiatrists have of themselves as social worker with prescription pad.

The specialist psychiatry of ID lies at the margins of even this marginal discipline and it seeks to justify its place amid the same pressures and preoccupations. This, along with the clinician's vocational desire to 'do better' for patients, is why definition, standardisation and measurement have become vital issues and why efforts behind such enterprises as the PIMRA, HoNOS-LD, the PAS-ADD family and the CANDID are so important, and will continue to be for some time yet. So, where are we after a quarter century of research effort and 15 years after Peter Sturmey's review (Sturmey et al. 1991)?

The fact that PAS-ADD, HoNOS-LD and CANDID exist at all is significant in itself, responses to an uncomfortable gap and designed with a special population in mind. Between them they have attempted to take account of the problems of communication, the need for simple measures that can track individual progress in treatment (and potentially act as indicators of performance by services), and the importance of assessing the wider personal and social problems that accompany mental health problems in planning effective packages of care. The developers of all three instruments have realised the importance of undertaking field trials that pay attention not only to vital psychometric properties such as reliability but also to the difficult problem (possibly even the 'deep problem') of *validity*. The PAS-ADD in particular has raised the problem that any specialist area of practice has to overcome: to what extent is it the same as the mainstream and to what extent is it truly different (Deb et al. 2001; Cooper et al. 2003; Sturmey et al. 2005)?

The psychiatry of ID looks like it may currently be caught on the horns of a dilemma. Take as an example the quintessential mental disorder, schizophrenia. It has been central to the way that the psychiatry of ID has made its case as a specialism that people with ID have mental illnesses, not *just like* anyone else but at a fundamental level *the same* as everyone else; the fact that it may be missed or misclassified an artefact of so-called 'diagnostic overshadowing' (Bernal and Hollins 1995). But the PAS-ADD has shown what many have long known, that some symptoms of schizophrenia rely on greater communicative ability to be reported than others, some symptoms such as delusional thinking may require more 'phenomenological interpretation' than is the case in the general psychiatric population, and some – in particular those, like passivity, constituting Schneider's First Rank Symptoms which lie at the core of the ICD-10 version of the diagnosis – may require greater levels of cognitive complexity to be experienced at all, let alone communicated. Aside from the considerations that went into designing the PAS-ADD, the literature looking at such fundamental issues delineating the precise nature of the symptoms of psychotic (and other) illnesses such as eating disorders in people with ID is vanishingly small and what there is is largely impressionistic (Gravestock

2003). It is hard to help feeling that research may be running ahead of itself and, to paraphrase the painful but apt cliché once beloved of politicians, it may soon be time to revisit some basics.

On the other hand, it is also true that the instruments reviewed here have been much neglected in research since their initial exploratory field trials, and in the areas of aetiological and outcome research in particular. In the end PAS-ADD, CANDID, HoNOS-LD and the others will survive only if they begin to tell us things we didn't already know about the mental health needs of people with ID and start sifting fact from fantasy in clinical practice (*how well does treatment X work?* say, or, *how heritable is this particular form of disorder?*). Until then we are less far forward than our growing body of research might lead us to think.

It could turn out, of course, that more of clinical practice than we would like to admit will elude efforts at objective definition or quantification. Perhaps it is the case that some important things *really are* just that bit too complicated, leaving us with little choice but to carry on as best we can regardless. While this should not stop us trying to do better, in doing so we need to resist the temptation (or pressure) to prematurely reduce the complexities of troubled lives to pale empirical shadows of the problems that real patients in the meantime bring to the clinic. Therefore, clinicians and researchers should collaborate to achieve greater standardisation of their assessment and diagnostic practices in relation to the complex psychopathology presented by people with intellectual disability.

NECESSARY STEPS TO BETTER SERVICES

- Specialist psychiatric assessment taking account of the communication and conceptualisation impairments of people with ID.
- Specialist psychiatric assessment that includes history-taking from the individual and informants, case note review and mental state examination. Ratings scales should be used as appropriate.
- Psychiatric diagnosis using recognised classification manuals and which may rely on modified diagnostic criteria in those with more severe ID.
- Rating instruments for psychopathology, needs, functioning and outcome may enable ongoing clinical practice assessment, diagnosis and psychometric research issues.

REFERENCES

Aman, M.G. and Singh, N.N. (1985) *The Aberrant Behavior Checklist*. East Aurora, NY: Slosson.

Aman, M.G., Watson, J.E., Singh, N.N., Turbott, S.H. and Wilsher, C.P. (1986) Psychometric and demographic characteristics of the Psychopathology Instrument for Mentally Retarded Adults. *Pharmacology Bulletin*, 22, 1972–1976.

Ballinger, B.R. and Reid, A.H. (1987) A standardised assessment of personality disorder in mental handicap. *British Journal of Psychiatry*, 150, 108–109.

Bernal, J. and Hollins, S. (1995) Psychiatric illness and learning disability: A dual diagnosis. *Advances in Psychiatric Treatment*, 1, 138–145.

Bouras, N. (2004) Assessment, diagnosis and treatment of schizophrenia spectrum disorders in people with intellectual disability. *World Psychiatry*, 3 (1), 40.

Bouras, N. and Hardy, S. (2002) The presentation and assessment of mental health problems in people with learning disabilities. *Learning Disability Practice*, 5, 33–38.

Bramston, P. and Fogarty, G. (2000) The assessment of emotional distress experienced by people with an intellectual disability: A study of different methodologies. *Research in Developmental Disabilities*, 21, 487–500.

Brewster, S.J. (2004) Putting words into their mouths? Interviewing people with learning disabilities and little/no speech. *British Journal of Learning Disabilities*, 32, 166–169.

Cooper, S.A., Melville, C.A. and Enfield, S. (2003) Psychiatric diagnosis, intellectual disabilities and Diagnostic Criteria for Psychiatric Disorders for Use with Adults with Learning Disabilities/Mental Retardation (DC-LD). *Journal of Intellectual Disability Research*, 47 (Suppl. 1), 3–15.

Deb, S., Matthews, T., Holt, G. and Bouras, N. (eds) (2001) *Practice Guidelines for the Assessment and Diagnosis of Mental Health Problems in Adults with Intellectual Disability.* Brighton, UK: Pavilion Publishing in association with the European Association of Mental Health in Mental Retardation.

Finlay, W.M.L. and Lyons, E. (2001) Methodological issues in interviewing and using self-report questionnaires with people with mental retardation. *Psychological Assessment*, 13, 319–335.

Flynn, A. (2008) Supporting people with learning disabilities on general psychiatric wards, PICUs and LSUs. In D.M. Beer, S.M. Pereira and C. Paton (eds), *Psychiatric Intensive Care* (2nd ed., pp. 202–219). Cambridge, UK: Cambridge University Press.

Flynn, A., Matthews, H. and Hollins, S. (2002) Validity of the diagnosis of personality disorder in adults with learning disability and severe behavioural problems. *British Journal of Psychiatry*, 180, 543–546.

Fulford, K.W.M. (1994) Closet logics: Hidden conceptual elements in the DSM and ICD classifications of mental disorders. In J.Z. Sadler, O.P. Wiggins and M.A. Schwartz (eds), *Philosophical Perspectives on Psychiatric Diagnostic Classification.* Baltimore, MD: Johns Hopkins University Press.

Gravestock, S. (1999) Adults with learning disabilities and mental health needs. *Tizard Learning Disability Review*, 4, 6–13.

Gravestock, S. (2003) Diagnosis and classification of eating disorders in adults with intellectual disability: The DC-LD approach. *Journal of Intellectual Disability Research*, 47 (Suppl. 1), 72–83.

Gravestock, S. and McCluskey, S. (2009) Assessment and management of eating disorders in adults with learning disabilities: The EDALD approach. Submitted for publication.

Gudjonsson, G.H. and Clare, I. (1986) Suggestibility in police interrogation: A social psychology model. *Social Behaviour*, 1, 83–104.

Holmes, N., Shah, A. and Wing, L. (1982) The Disability Assessment Schedule: A brief screening device for use with the mentally retarded. *Psychological Medicine*, 12, 879–890.

Mactavish, J.B., Mahon, M.J. and Lutfiyya, Z.M. (2000) 'I can speak for myself': Involving individuals with intellectual disabilities as research participants. *Mental Retardation*, 38, 216–227.

Matson, J.L., Kazdin, A.E. and Senatore, V. (1984) Psychometric properties of the Psychopathology Instrument for Mentally Retarded Adults. *Applied Research in Mental Retardation*, 5, 881–889.

Moss, S.C., Patel, P., Prosser, H., Goldberg, D., Simpson, N., Rowe, S. and Lucchino, R. (1993) Psychiatric morbidity in older people with moderate and severe learning disability. Part 1: Development and reliability of the patient interview (PAS-ADD). *British Journal of Psychiatry*, 163, 471–480.

Moss, S.C., Prosser, H., Costello, H., Simpson, N., Patel, P., Rowe, S., Turner, S. and Hatton, C. (1998) Reliability and validity of the PAS-ADD Checklist for detecting psychiatric disorders in adults with intellectual disability. *Journal of Intellectual Disability Research*, 42, 173–183.

Moss, S., Prosser, H. and Goldberg, D. (1996a) Validity of the schizophrenia diagnosis of the Psychiatric Assessment Schedule for Adults with Developmental Disability (PAS-ADD). *British Journal of Psychiatry*, 168, 359–367.

Moss, S., Prosser, H., Ibbotson, B. and Goldberg, D. (1996b) Respondent and informant accounts of psychiatric symptoms in a sample of patients with learning disability. *Journal of Intellectual Disability Research*, 40, 457–465.

Pickard, M. and Gravestock, S. (2001) HoNOS-LD as a measurement of long term change. *Abstracts of Faculty for Psychiatry of Learning Disability Annual Residential Meeting* (p. 4). London: Royal College of Psychiatrists.

Pilgrim, J.A., Mellers, J.D., Boothby, H.A. and Mann, A.H. (1990) Inter-rater and temporal reliability of the Standardised Assessment of Personality and the influence of informant characteristics. *Psychological Medicine*, 23, 779–786.

Powell, R. (2003) Psychometric properties of the Beck Depression Inventory and the Zung Self Rating Depression Scale in adults with mental retardation. *Mental Retardation*, 41, 88–95.

Prosser, H. and Bromley, J. (1998) Interviewing people with intellectual disabilities. In E. Emerson, C. Hatton, J. Bromley and A. Craine (eds), *Clinical Psychology and People with Intellectual Disabilities* (pp. 99–113). Chichester, UK: Wiley.

Reiss, S. (1990) Prevalence of dual diagnosis in community-based day programs in the Chicago metropolitan area. *American Journal on Mental Retardation*, 94, 578–585.

Roy, A., Matthews, H., Clifford, P., Fowler, V. and Martin, D.M. (2002) Health of the Nation Outcome Scales for People with Learning Disabilities (HoNOS-LD). *British Journal of Psychiatry*, 180, 61–66.

Senatore, V., Matson, J.L. and Kazdin, A.E. (1985) An inventory to assess psychopathology in the mentally retarded. *American Journal of Mental Deficiency*, 89, 459–466.

Sigelman, C., Budd, E., Winer, J., Schoenrock, C. and Martin, P. (1982) Evaluating alternative techniques of questioning mentally retarded persons. *American Journal of Mental Deficiency*, 86, 511–518.

Slater, L. (2004) Lost in the mall: The false memory experiment. In *Opening Skinner's Box: Great Psychological Experiments of the Twentieth Century* (pp. 182–204). London: Bloomsbury.

Sturmey, P. (1999) Concepts, classification and assessment. In N. Bouras (ed.), *Psychiatric and Behavioural Disorders in Developmental Disabilities and Mental Retardation* (pp. 3–17). Cambridge, UK: Cambridge University Press.

Sturmey, P. and Ley, T. (1990) The Psychopathology Instrument for Mentally Retarded Adults: Internal consistencies and relationship to behaviour problems. *British Journal of Psychiatry*, 156, 428–430.

Sturmey, P., Newton, J.T., Cowley, A., Bouras, N. and Holt, G. (2005) The PAS-ADD Checklist: Independent replication of its psychometric properties in a community sample. *British Journal of Psychiatry*, 186, 319–323.

Sturmey, P., Reed, J. and Corbett, J. (1991) Psychometric assessment of psychiatric disorders in people with learning disabilities (mental handicap): A review of measures. *Psychological Medicine*, 21, 143–155.

Tyrer, P., Oliver-Africano, P.C., Ahmed, Z., Bouras, N., Cooray, S., Deb, S., Murphy, D.,

Hare, M., Meade, M., Reece, B., Kramo, K., Bhaumik, S., Harley, D., Regan, A., Thomas, D., Rao, B., North, B., Eliahoo, J., Karatela, S., Soni, A. and Crawford, M. (2008) Risperidone, haloperidol, and placebo in the treatment of aggressive challenging behaviour in patients with intellectual disability: A randomised controlled trial. *Lancet*, 371, 57–63.

Watson, J.E., Aman, M.G. and Singh, N.N. (1988) The Psychopathology Instrument for Mentally Retarded Adults: Psychometric characteristics, factor structure, and relationship to subject characteristics. *Research in Developmental Disabilities*, 9, 277–290.

Xenitidis, K., Thornicroft, G., Leese, M., Slade, M., Fotiadou, M., Philp, H., Sayer, J., Harris, E., McGee, D. and Murphy, D.G. (2000) Reliability and validity of the CANDID – a needs assessment instrument for adults with learning disabilities and mental health problems. *British Journal of Psychiatry*, 176, 473–478.

CHAPTER FIVE

Service use and outcomes

Colin Hemmings

INTRODUCTION

In many developed countries such as the UK there have been rapid moves away from institutionalized care towards community care for people with intellectual disabilities (ID). This has been in the context of changes in policy regarding the health and social care for people with ID (see Chapter 1). Over the same period it has become increasingly recognized that people with ID are actually more likely to have additional mental disorders than people of typical IQ (Deb et al. 2001; Cooper et al. 2007). A significant proportion of people with ID in the community therefore have coexisting mental health problems causing much morbidity, carer burden and health and social care service costs. Despite this situation there remains a serious lack of evidence on the effectiveness of mental health services for them.

One of the great needs at the start of the new era in community care for people with ID and mental health problems was to collect data and research the services provided for them. For this purpose the integrated clinical service of Mental Health in Learning Disabilities (MHiLD) (see Chapter 1) together with Estia Centre staff devised and used a specially created form, the *Mental Health Assessment & Information Rating Profile* (Bouras and Drummond 1989). This collected information on each service user referred to the allied specialist mental health service for people with ID in South East London. Information was recorded on multiple variables, including demographic details, medication, medical and family history, course of illness, and daytime activities. Over the course of the following years a great many health service research studies have been carried out on the basis of this information kept on sequential referrals to the clinical service. The health service research studies have been wide-ranging, including information on referrals and pathways to care, the characteristics of service users referred and their consumption of services. These studies have also provided a foundation to look at the crucial question of whether there should be specialist as well as generic provision for this population. Studies have looked at in-patient care and more recently community care, particularly for those with ID and more severe mental illness who may need at times more intensive input to maintain them in the community. This chapter will provide an overview of how the health service delivery research output from the Estia Centre evolved over the past 25 five years.

REFERRALS/PATHWAYS TO CARE

Bouras et al. (2003) published data based on the information collected on 752 new referrals to the specialist mental health in ID clinical service allied to the Estia Centre in South East London between 1983 and 2001 using the Assessment and Information Profile. The long time span of the referrals took in the closure of the two major asylums and the move of people with ID to community settings. Over the period studied more non-white clients and more with mild ID were referred. This reflected the changing demographics of the local population. More referrals were made overall as the service became more established, probably reflecting greater recognition of people with mild ID and their needs in the community. Later referrals were also more likely to have a psychiatric diagnosis. This may have resulted from increased referrer awareness or improved diagnostic assessments, or it could simply have been true findings of an increased prevalence of mental disorders in those referred.

There was a marked increase in the proportion living independently. There was no change in the prevalence rates of autism among those referred (up to 2001). It would be interesting to see if this finding would still apply to more recent referrals given the raised consciousness of autism in professionals as well as in lay opinion and the improved screening and diagnostic instruments for autistic spectrum disorders. This study also found a decrease in those with generalized epilepsy, possibly reflecting the recognition over time that people with ID and epilepsy should access general medical services rather than specialist mental health services. There was a decrease in those admitted to a generic mental health unit after the first assessment. This may have reflected improved community monitoring and treatment available from the service and also later on the commissioning of a specialist unit locally for people with ID and mental health problems (opened in 1999).

Maitland et al. (2006) looked at pathways to care among broadly this same group of referrals (*n* = 791) to the clinical service between 1983 and 2003. The study compared referrals from primary care/social services and secondary care services (generic mental health services). Secondary care referrals were more likely to have schizophrenia spectrum disorders, personality disorders and mild ID, and were more likely to be hospital in-patients and to be of Asian ethnic origin. Primary care/social services' referrals were more likely to have dementia or no psychiatric diagnosis at all and more likely to live in supported housing. This suggested that the specialist clinical service was acting on two different levels: secondary when receiving from primary care and tertiary when receiving referrals from secondary care of people with more severe mental disorders such as schizophrenia and personality disorder.

Tsakanikos et al. (2007b) carried out a similar study of pathways but this time focused on adults referred with autistic spectrum disorders (ASD). They examined patterns of change in referral trends, types of mental health diagnoses and treatment to specialist mental health services in South London from 1983 to 2000 in 137 adults with ASD and ID. The majority of the cases (58.4%) did not have any additional diagnosable mental illness. Schizophrenia was the most frequent additional diagnosis followed by depression, adjustment reaction and anxiety. There was a significant change in the rate of referrals, an increase in the diagnosable psychiatric disorders over time and a significant reduction of medication at time of referral. There were no significant changes in the use of other therapeutic interventions. Again, it was found that the proportion of participants living independently had increased.

Tsakanikos et al. (submitted) explored ethnic factors in those referred to the specialist mental health service. There was an under-representation of referrals from ethnic minority groups relative to the local population. However, there was a significantly increased prevalence of schizophrenia spectrum disorder among black and other non-white people referred. In addition, black participants were more likely to have an autistic spectrum disorder. Referrals of ethnic minority groups were considerably younger than white referrals, and less likely to be in supported residences. The authors discussed the range of possible factors that might have accounted for these ethnic differences in diagnoses and care pathways.

CHARACTERISTICS OF SERVICE USERS AND CONSUMPTION OF SERVICES

Kon and Bouras (1997) conducted one of the earliest studies of community services. They followed the progress of 74 individuals with ID resettled from a mental handicap asylum in Kent. They assessed the cohort prior to discharge, one year after resettlement and again after five years. Overall the resettlement was reported to have been successful, for example, as measured by service user satisfaction with the new accommodation. The study, though, found deficiencies in daytime activities and day care for those resettled. It found that the prevalence of mental disorders and behavioural problems did not significantly change. There had been a view that institutionalization was perhaps the only major determinant of these problems (Bouras and Holt 2004). This study therefore helped to challenge the prevailing view that community care in itself was going to solve all the problems of institutionalization, particularly if community care was not resourced or researched adequately.

Bouras et al. (2004) produced important evidence that people with ID and mental health problems have more complex needs than those with mental health problems in the wider population. In this study the authors compared clinical, functional, and social factors in patients with mild ID and schizophrenia spectrum disorders (SSD) attending the specialist mental health service for people with ID in South East London, with a control group of patients without ID but with SSD attending a generic adult mental health (GAMH) outpatient clinic. A total of 106 patients with SSP (53 with ID and 53 from GAMH) were assessed on psychopathological symptoms, functioning scales and quality of life. Increases in observable psychopathology and 'negative' schizophrenic symptoms, and decreased functional abilities were observed in the group with ID when compared to the GAMH group. Those dually diagnosed with ID and SSP appeared therefore to be more debilitated by the co-occurring disorder than those with the same disorder but without ID. Despite this, their quality of life overall was not significantly different to the GAMH group, perhaps contrary to what might have been expected given their added disabilities. Similar evidence highlighting the more complex needs of those with ID as well as schizophrenia relative to those with schizophrenia alone have been found in a recent Australian study (Morgan et al. 2008).

Tsakanikos et al. (2007a) examined behaviour management problems as predictors of psychotropic medication, use of psychiatric consultation and in-patient admission in a group of 66 adults with pervasive developmental disorder (PDD) and ID and 99 controls matched in age, gender and level of ID. Data were collected from retrospective case review. Overall, people with PDD had higher rates of most behaviour problems and more frequent use of anti-psychotic medications than matched controls. Logistic regression analyses showed that physical aggression and other problems such as pestering staff independently predicted use of anti-psychotics and further involvement of the mental health services. Having a PDD diagnosis was associated with increased rates of admissions to an in-patient unit. The results suggested that externalizing problem behaviours in adults with autism could predict the type of treatment intervention received.

Spiller et al. (2007) carried out a retrospective case review of consumption of mental health services in a sample of 115 service users with ID referred to the clinical service between 1996 and 2001. The authors constructed a service consumption index based on the number of outpatient clinics attended, contacts with the community psychiatric nurses, home visits by a psychiatrist and the number of admissions. This index was used to divide the sample into two groups, heavy and light service users. Those with schizophrenia and a greater number of affective/neurotic symptoms were more likely to be heavy service users. In logistic regression analysis, service users with schizophrenia were more than seven times more likely to be heavy service users than those without this diagnosis. A significant association was also found between those likely to be heavy service users and those receiving input from the local Behavioural Support team, reflecting the clinical and service importance of challenging behaviours. Those with heavy service use were also found to be more likely to be those who needed more long-term care.

Age, living situation and the degree of ID were not found to be significant predictors of service consumption. The results suggested that a small proportion of service users consumed almost half of the service resources, a similar finding to similar research studies in generic adult mental health services. This study adapted a scale used in generic research known as the Service Consumption Score (Tansella et al. 1986). The study also showed that a substantial proportion of the service resources had been devoted to one-off assessments. This finding suggested that clinicians in specialist ID mental health services may often assess individuals with ID who do not necessarily have a diagnosable mental illness or challenging behaviours requiring ongoing psychiatric input.

MORE INTENSIVE SERVICES

Owing at least in part to the studies described above, the general availabliity of evidence about community services for people with ID and mental health problems is now gradually improving (Hemmings 2008). Once community services were established there was increasing interest as to how these might need to evolve. One question has been, is there a need for more intensive services for some people with ID and mental health problems who are at risk of distressing and costly in-patient admissions? Cowley et al. (2005) looked at predictive factors for psychiatric inpatient admissions within a cohort of 752 adults with ID living in community settings in South East London. This study showed that a diagnosis of schizophrenia spectrum disorders (as well as mild ID) in its large sample was associated with admission. In an analysis of a subsample, physical aggression also independently predicted admission. There was no overrepresentation of those admitted by gender or by ethnicity. The authors suggested that improvements in community care might decrease the need for some of these admissions and called for evaluations of assertive outreach-type community services.

It can be argued that people with ID with coexisting mental health problems have not had the same access to developments in mainstream community mental health service delivery that have occurred in recent times. Following the introduction of assertive outreach, home treatment and crisis resolution services and other service innovations for the wider population with more severe mental illness research interest began to grow in more intensive services for those with ID and dual diagnosis (Hassiotis et al. 2003). Martin et al. (2005) reported an exploratory study of assertive community treatment for people with ID and mental health problems. This was of particular note as it was a randomized controlled trial, albeit with a small sample but one of the only examples of studies using this methodology in the ID mental health service field. They compared their Assertive Community Treatment in ID (ACT-ID) model with 'standard community treatment' in a sample of 20 participants with mild or moderate ID and a coexisting mental illness (schizophrenia spectrum or affective disorder). People with challenging behaviours but no diagnosable mental illnesses were excluded in this study. Those with severe ID were also excluded, as were those who needed immediate intensive treatment. Participants were assessed at baseline and again at six months after beginning treatment.

The ACT-type model used in this study (ACT-ID) was defined only in terms of contact with professionals. ACT-ID was defined as contact with two staff members as often as required. Contact with one staff member no more than once weekly was defined as 'standard community treatment'. This study showed no major differences between the 'assertive' and 'standard' groups using a range of outcome measures. Both standard and assertive groups showed decreased unmet needs and carer burden and increased functioning and quality of life. However, there were no statistically significant differences between the two treatment groups. The authors argued that their results did not indicate that ACT in people with ID is clearly ineffective. Instead this study had highlighted the difficulties in the research methodology and in the implementation of ACT in ID services.

A similar study published around the same time by Oliver et al. (2005) also did not find significant differences in outcomes for service users with more intensive input, but the researchers came against the same methodological difficulties (Chaplin 2006). Problems in developing and evaluating ACT-type models for people with ID have included the fidelity of the models to the original ACT model and a lack of distinction between them and the control services. The definition of ACT used in the ACT-ID study was significantly different from the original ACT model and also different from studies of mainstream community mental health services in the UK. The treatment received from control services in the ACT-ID studies was similar to the intervention ('assertive') services and this may have accounted for the lack of difference in outcomes.

In order to take this research forward it was recognized that qualitative studies were necessary first to provide a foundation (Chaplin 2006). Following the ACT-ID study, therefore, further work examined the opinion of a multidisciplinary group of clinicians regarding ACT in people with ID. This found much inconsistency regarding the use of the model (Hemmings et al. 2008b). It showed that it was probably too difficult to evaluate intensive service models such as ACT in people with ID and mental health problems when there was so little consensus as to its definition and implementation for this specific service user group. Furthermore, there were not even any previously reported standards of what routine services should provide for this service user group.

This study further showed the need for qualitative and quantitative studies that went still further back in the research design continuum. Focusing on the severely mentally ill (those with psychosis) with ID also allowed a clearer comparison with similar research in people with severe mental illness but without ID. The aim of these studies was to establish what should be the components of routine and more intensive services for people with ID and psychosis in the community. This research utilized the opinions and experiences of service users and their carers as well as professionals. The studies included a systematic consultation of multidisciplinary professionals using a three-round Delphi exercise (Hemmings et al. 2009b). This technique had been used to look at expert opinion of mental health services for the general population but not before for services for people with ID. Participants for this study ($n = 52$) were recruited nationally. They rated their views on the importance of 139 items for the care of adults with psychosis and ID. These included 85 routine service components, 23 service user characteristics for those needing a more intensive service and 31 more intensive service components. Forty-nine out of the 52 participants completed all three rounds of the Delphi consultation. Consensus of opinion (= 80% agreement as essential) was obtained on 18 of the routine service components, nine of the service user characteristics and five of the more intensive service components. The routine service components considered essential could be broadly considered under a need for a focused approach on the service user and their illness (e.g. *monitoring of mental state*) and the added need to work within the wider context of the service user with psychosis and ID (e.g. *access to social, leisure or occupational activities*). Five of the more intensive service components were considered to be essential (e.g. *can react to a crisis that day*). However, the routine service components considered essential already contained many components such as *out-of-hours support* and *crisis plans* also relevant to more intensive services. These findings can be used to develop further the evidence base for services in the community for this user group and to assist in the preparation of much-needed service evaluation studies.

The early literature had been dominated by inpatient service descriptions rather than regarding services in the community, reflecting where most care was provided before the most recent decades. Case studies (e.g. Hemmings and Greig 2007) have described the importance of specialist units in certain complex cases. In a field short of evidence, though, three more recent studies of in-patient admissions have been conducted at the Estia Centre.

Xenitidis et al. (1999) studied the first 64 patients admitted to the Mental Impairment Evaluation and Treatment Service (MIETS) in South London following its opening. MIETS is an in-patient unit for the assessment and treatment of people with ID who exhibit challenging behaviour (CB). Those with challenging behaviours have been the most difficult-to-place group and use a large amount of service resources. A within-subject comparison research design was used in this study. Demographic and clinical data were obtained from case records and the effectiveness of interventions was evaluated by comparing the number of incidents of challenging behaviour, the use of seclusion, and the place of residence before and after the inpatient intervention. Only 10 (17.5%) of the patients had been admitted from community facilities, but 48 (84.2%) of the patients were discharged to community placements. The in-patient admission to this specialist unit also significantly reduced the frequency and severity of challenging behaviours. The authors concluded that the MIETS (and potentially then other similar specialist in-patient units) was an effective treatment model for people with ID and challenging behaviours.

Xenitidis et al. (2004) then evaluated the effectiveness of a specialist ID mental health in-patient unit for people with ID and mental health problems and also reported on the utilization of generic and specialist in-patient services (see also Chapter 1). All patients who had been admitted ($n = 84$) to the specialist unit from 1999 to 2002 were evaluated on admission and immediately after discharge on a number of outcome measures. In addition, they were compared with those admitted to general adult mental health units covering the same catchment area of South East London. Significant improvements in immediate outcomes (on discharge) were demonstrated within the specialist unit cohort on measures including psychopathology, global level of functioning, behavioural impairment and severity of mental illness. The specialist unit patients had a longer in-patient stay but were less likely to be discharged to out-of-area residential placements. Again this provided evidence that specialist units are an effective care option for this group of people.

This study was then expanded upon with an extended period of study and thus much larger sample (Hemmings et al. 2009a). The study was further developed by excluding individuals admitted to both the specialist unit and generic wards from the statistical analysis and placing them in a separate group to make three groups for comparison. This was to prevent service users appearing in both exclusive groups and increasing the risk of Type II errors in the analysis.

Socio-demographic and clinical characteristics of 154 consecutive admissions over a five-and-a-half-year period between 1999 and 2004 were recorded. Key differences in this more highly powered study were found in psychiatric diagnosis, residence type and discharge destination between individuals using generic and specialist provision. Significantly more adults admitted to generic units were diagnosed with an affective disorder. Length of stay was significantly longer for specialist unit admissions. Admissions to the specialist unit were significantly more likely to reside with family prior to admission and admissions to generic units were significantly more likely to come from 'other' forms of residence such as hostels, prison and 'no fixed abode'. At discharge the proportion of those admitted to the specialist unit who resided with their families reduced. At the same time the proportion of those living in supported accommodation increased, although compared to those admitted to generic units they were still significantly more likely to return to the family home. This research suggested that specialist in-patient provision may be crucial in helping mainstream services meet the needs of individuals with ID and mental health problems. In-patient services for people with ID and mental health problems have also recently been studied by Alexander et al. (2001) and Hall et al. (2006) (see Chapter 1).

STRENGTHS AND LIMITATIONS

The Estia Centre research output has had a great many strengths. Perhaps the major one and the reason for its wider influence has been its strong focus on mental disorders and challenging behaviours rather than on the primary health care or social care of people with ID. Primary health and social care service delivery to people with ID and the evaluation of it is also of critical importance, but it was recognized that specialist mental health services should focus on their core role and the ongoing development and improvement of expertise in this area. This recognition was not always shared by other specialist ID services in the UK, particularly at the time of inception of the Estia Centre and its allied clinical service in South London. Over this time there has also been ongoing debate about whether standard classification systems should be used in clinical practice and in research.

The adoption of standardized diagnostic criteria, notably ICD-10 (WHO 1992) has allowed greater comparisons of the research studies described in this chapter with similar research in the ID field and with the much larger research base from mental health service research for the wider population. There have also been contributions to the ongoing debate regarding the concepts and overlap of mental disorders versus challenging behaviour for people with ID (Hemmings et al. 2006, 2008a; Hemmings 2007). The challenging behaviour of people with ID not within the context of mental disorders or within the social care model has been extensively studied by researchers including Allen (2003), Mansell (Department of Health 2007), Emerson (1995), Hatton (2002) and Sturmey (1994).

Estia Centre staff encouraged a culture of research, locally, nationally and internationally. One of the strengths of the published research output is how it has often been linked in with various and substantial training initiatives (see Chapter 8), conferences, texts for non-specialists and wider policy debates. The health service research also, while practical and of great use to clinicians and commissioners, has always been grounded in conceptual frameworks (e.g. Moss et al. 2000).

Inevitably there are a number of limitations to the research. There have been ongoing problems with recruitment of people with ID for research, now exacerbated by the properly increased standards of ethical approval required to undertake research with vulnerable people where capacity to consent to take part may often be impaired. This has meant that sample sizes in some studies such as the ACT-ID trial have often been lower than would have been hoped. There have been relatively few multi-site studies, which can affect the generalizability of some of the research findings. This potential generalizability problem is magnified as the clinical service in South East London provides care in a highly disadvantaged inner-city area with high rates of social problems.

Some of the studies have been retrospective with their attendant potential for bias. Prospective studies and intervention studies will be increasingly important now the research base is more established. Some of the earlier studies were based on how the services provided are used by people with ID rather than on their actual needs.

It is true also that there remains a dearth of outcome studies. Furthermore, the outcomes sometimes used have not been as wide as it is currently recognized they should be. For example, it is now widely accepted that outcomes should include such measures as carer burden, service user satisfaction, quality of life and an economic evaluation of existing or new service delivery.

Another limitation in hindsight is that some of the earlier studies were carried out without the benefit of the improvements in rating instruments and reliability of assessments over this period. However, all of these limitations perhaps have only been made evident with the experience of the work that has already taken place.

CONCLUSION

People with both ID and mental health problems are among the most vulnerable and socially excluded in society. Yet in general there has been far too little attention to the evaluation of services they currently receive and to the identification of the specific service components they might need. UK government policy in recent years has promoted the use of mainstream services wherever possible for people with ID. However, this policy has not been particularly evidence-based. Ongoing problems have been faced by people with ID and mental health problems in accessing generic mental health services adequate for their needs (Bouras and Holt 2000). A crucial question has been, do people with ID and mental health problems do better in specialist services or in generic services? As there has been such a paucity of research to base services on, there remains no conclusive evidence to favour the use of either (Chaplin 2004). Research into health service delivery conducted at the Estia Centre has at least helped to provide the foundation to address the specialist versus generic services question (see Chapter 1).

The context of this research work was that very few others had the foresight and determination to evaluate from the outset of deinstitutionalization what their services were providing and what their service users needed. The Estia Centre staff in the 1980s showed great application in collecting data on their referrals ever since their inception. They were committed from an early stage to an evidence-based practice. Owing to this vision and perspicacity during that period, Estia Centre researchers have provided a major contribution to the rapid expansion of the evidence base into health service delivery for people with ID and mental health problems. Ongoing research is vital to determine what mental health services should be like for this disadvantaged service user group and how these services should evolve.

NECESSARY STEPS TO BETTER SERVICES

- Make the service evidence-based, with a research culture and active participation in research locally.
- Ensure that the service delivery is conceptually guided to provide a theoretical foundation for its clinical aims.
- Run or contribute to allied training programmes for both carers and clinicians.
- Focus on specific service components rather than service configurations.

- Use standardized criteria for diagnosis and validated rating instruments.
- Compare how service users do in the specialist service and local generic services.
- Use a wide range of outcomes including user satisfaction and carer burden as well as psychopathology.
- Do not try to separate services neatly into those for people with diagnosable mental illness and those with challenging behaviours.
- Research the characteristics of the service users being referred and their consumption of the service resources.
- Research which needs of service users and carers are not being met by the service.
- Stay focused on the core roles of a specialist mental health service, while trying to achieve the best possible interfaces with other services taking the lead in social and general health care.

REFERENCES

Alexander, R.T., Piachaud, J. and Singh, I. (2001) Two districts, two models: In-patient care in the psychiatry of learning disability. *British Journal of Developmental Disabilities*, 47, 105–110.

Allen, D. (ed.) (2003) *Ethical approaches to physical intervention: Responding to Challenging Behaviour in Persons with Intellectual Disabilities*. Kidderminster, UK: British Institute of Learning Disabilities.

Bouras, N. and Drummond, K. (1989) Community psychiatric services in mental handicap. *Health Trends*, 21, 72.

Bouras, N., Cowley, A., Holt, G., Newton, J.T. and Sturmey, P. (2003) Referral trends of people with intellectual disabilities and psychiatric disorders. *Journal of Intellectual Disability Research*, 47, 439–446.

Bouras, N. and Holt, G. (2000) The planning and provision of psychiatric services for people with mental retardation. In M.G. Gelder, J.J. Lopez-Ibor, Jr and C. Andreasen (eds), *The New Oxford Textbook of Psychiatry* (pp. 2007–2012). Oxford, UK: Oxford University Press.

Bouras, N. and Holt, G. (2004) Mental health services for adults with learning disabilities. *British Journal of Psychiatry*, 184, 291–292.

Bouras, N., Martin, G., Leese, M., Vanstraelen, M., Holt, G., Thomas, C., Hindler, C. and Boardman, J. (2004) Schizophrenia-spectrum psychoses in people with and without intellectual disability. *Journal of Intellectual Disability Research*, 48 (6), 548–555.

Chaplin, R. (2004) General psychiatric services for adults with intellectual disability and mental illness. *Journal of Intellectual Disability Research*, 48, 1–10.

Chaplin, R. (2006) Assertive outreach for people with intellectual disability and mental disorders. *Journal of Intellectual Disability Research*, 50, 615–616.

Cooper, S.-A., Smiley, E., Morrison, J., Williamson, A. and Allan, L. (2007) Mental ill-health in adults with intellectual disabilities: Prevalence and associated factors. *British Journal of Psychiatry*, 190, 27–35.

Cowley, A., Newton, J., Sturmey, P., Bouras, N. and Holt, G. (2005) Psychiatric inpatient admissions of adults with intellectual disabilities: Predictive factors. *American Journal on Mental Retardation*, 110, 216–225.

Deb, S., Thomas, M. and Bright, C. (2001) Mental disorder in adults with intellectual disability: Prevalence of functional psychiatric illness among a community based population aged between 16 and 64 years. *Journal of Intellectual Disability Research*, 45, 495–505.

Department of Health (2007) *Services for People with Learning Disabilities and Challenging Behaviour or Mental Health Needs*. London: HMSO.

Emerson, E. (1995) *Challenging Behaviour: Analysis and Intervention in People with Learning Difficulties*. Cambridge, UK: Cambridge University Press.

Hall, I., Parkes, C., Samuels, S. and Hassiotis, A. (2006) Working across boundaries: Clinical outcomes for an integrated mental health service for people with intellectual disabilities. *Journal of Intellectual Disability Research*, 50, 598–607.

Hassiotis, A., Tyrer, P., Oliver, P. (2003) Psychiatric assertive outreach and learning disability services. *Advances in Psychiatric Treatment*, 9, 368–373.

Hatton, C. (2002). Psychosocial interventions for adults with intellectual disabilities and mental health problems: A review. *Journal of Mental Health*, 11, 357–373.

Hemmings, C.P. (2007). The relationships between challenging behaviours and psychiatric disorders in people with severe intellectual disabilities. In N. Bouras and G. Holt (eds), *Psychiatric and Behavioural Disorders in Intellectual and Developmental Disabilities* (2nd ed., pp. 62–75). Cambridge, UK: Cambridge University Press.

Hemmings, C.P. (2008) Community services for people with intellectual disabilities and mental health problems. *Current Opinion in Psychiatry*, 21, 459–462.

Hemmings, C.P, Gravestock, M., Pickard, M. and Bouras, N. (2006) Psychiatric symptoms and problem behaviours in people with intellectual disabilities. *Journal of Intellectual Disability Research*, 50, 269–276.

Hemmings, C.P. and Greig, A. (2007) Mental health or learning disabilities? The use of a specialist inpatient unit for a man with learning disabilities, schizophrenia and vascular dementia. *Advances in Mental Health and Learning Disabilities*, 1, 32–35.

Hemmings, C.P., O'Hara, J., McCarthy, J., Holt, G., Coster, F., Costello, H., Hammond, R., Xenitidis, K. and Bouras, N. (2009a) Comparison of adults with intellectual disabilities and mental health problems admitted to specialist and generic inpatient units. *British Journal of Learning Disabilities*, 37 (2), 123–128.

Hemmings, C.P, Tsakanikos, E., Underwood, L., Holt, G. and Bouras, N. (2008a) Clinical predictors of severe behavioural problems in people with intellectual disabilities. *Social Psychiatry and Psychiatric Epidemiology*, 127, 370–379.

Hemmings, C.P., Underwood, L. and Bouras, N. (2008b) Assertive Community Treatment for people with intellectual disabilities and mental health problems. *Psychiatric Services*, 59, 936–937.

Hemmings, C.P., Underwood, L. and Bouras, N. (2009b) Services in the community for adults with psychosis and intellectual disabilities: A Delphi consultation of professionals' views. *Journal of Intellectual Disability Research*, 53 (7), 677–684.

Kon, Y. and Bouras, N. (1997) Psychiatric follow up and health services utilisation for people with learning disabilities. *British Journal of Developmental Disabilities*, 84, 20–26.

Maitland, C., Tsakanikos, E., Holt, G., O'Hara, J. and Bouras, N. (2006) Mental health service provision for adults with intellectual disability: Sources of referrals, clinical characteristics and pathways to care. *Primary Care Mental Health*, 4, 99–106.

Martin, G., Costello, H., Leese, M., Slade, M. and Bouras, N. (2005) An exploratory study of assertive community treatment for people with intellectual disability and psychiatric disorders: Conceptual, clinical, and service issues. *Journal of Intellectual Disability Research*, 49, 516–524.

Morgan, V.A., Leonard, H., Bourke, J. and Jablensky, A. (2008) Intellectual disability co-occurring with schizophrenia and other psychiatric illness: Population-based study. *British Journal of Psychiatry*, 193, 364–372.

Moss, S., Bouras, N. and Holt, G. (2000) Mental health services for people with intellectual disability: A conceptual framework. *Journal of Intellectual Disability Research*, 44, 97–107.

Oliver, P., Piachaud, J., Tyrer, P., Regan, A., Dack, M., Alexander, R., Bakala, A., Cooray, S., Done, D.J. and Rao, B. (2005) Randomized controlled trial of assertive community treatment in intellectual disability: The TACTILD study. *Journal of Intellectual Disability Research*, 49, 507–515.

Spiller, M.J., Costello, H., Bramley, A., Bouras, N., Martin, G., Tsakanikos, E. and Holt, G. (2007) Consumption of mental health services by people with intellectual disabilities. *Journal of Applied Research in Intellectual Disabilities*, 20, 430–438.

Sturmey, P. (1994) Assessing the functions of aberrant behaviours: A review of psychometric instruments. *Journal of Autism and Developmental Disorders*, 24, 293–304.

Tansella, M., Micciolo, R., Balestrieri, M. and Gavioli, I. (1986) High and long-term users of the mental health services. *Social Psychiatry and Psychiatric Epidemiology*, 21, 96–103.

Tsakanikos, E., Costello, H., Holt, G., Sturmey, P. and Bouras, N. (2007a) Behaviour management problems as predictors of psychotropic medication and use of psychiatric services in adults with autism. *Journal of Autism and Developmental Disorders*, 37 (6), 1080–1085.

Tsakanikos, E., Maitland, C.H., Holt, G., O'Hara, J., Hemmings, C.P., McCarthy, J., Fearon, P. and Bouras, N. (submitted for publication) The role of ethnicity in clinical psychopathology and care pathways of adults with intellectual disabilities.

Tsakanikos, E., Sturmey, P., Costello, H., Holt, G. and Bouras, N. (2007b) Referral trends in mental health services for adults with autism and intellectual disability. *Autism*, 11, 9–17.

World Health Organisation (1992) *The ICD-10 Classification of Mental and Behavioural Disorders: Clinical Descriptions and Diagnostic Guidelines*. Geneva: WHO.

Xenitidis, K., Gratsa, A., Bouras, N., Hammond, R., Ditchfield, H., Holt, G., Martin, G. and Brooks, D. (2004) Psychiatric inpatient care for adults with intellectual disabilities: Generic or specialist units? *Journal of Intellectual Disability Research*, 48, 1–11.

Xenitidis, K.I., Henry, J., Russell, A.J., Ward, A. and Murphy, D.G.M. (1999) An inpatient treatment model for adults with mild intellectual disability and challenging behaviour. *Journal of Intellectual Disability Research*, 43, 128–134.

CHAPTER SIX

Neuroimaging and genetic syndromes

Duncan Harding and Dene Robertson

INTRODUCTION

Neuroimaging technology has leapt forward in the past 20 years. Neuro-imaging techniques have had a dramatic impact in psychiatry research, and this impact is clearly demonstrated in the field of intellectual disability (ID). In addition, it has become significantly more available as a clinical tool, such that both magnetic resonance imaging (MRI) and computerised tomography (CT) have become a regular and usual part of clinical mental health practice. This chapter reviews currently available neuroimaging techniques, illustrates their research applications in representative neurodevelopmental disorders associated with ID, and considers the role of neuroimaging and genetic screening in the Behavioural Genetics Clinic at the Maudsley Hospital – a specialist clinic for adults who may have neurodevelopmental disorders.

NEUROIMAGING TECHNIQUES

Computerised tomography scanning

CT scanning was developed from X-ray technology, and involves imaging multi-angled thin tissue slices that are combined on a computer to generate images of slices through the body. CT is cheaper, faster and more readily available to general hospitals than MRI – this makes it the investigation of choice for certain acute brain investigations, such as trauma or haemorrhage. CT demonstrates bone and bleeds well, but it has the disadvantage of exposing the patient to large doses of ionising radiation and is not as good as MRI at imaging soft tissue, or tissue that borders thick bone.

CT scanning techniques were used in early neuroimaging psychiatric research and helped to demonstrate the enlargement of lateral ventricles that is consistently found in groups of people who suffer from schizophrenia (e.g., Chua and McKenna 1995). In addition, CT technology was employed to investigate a range of other neurological and psychiatric conditions. For example, chronic alcohol use was found to give rise to enlarged ventricles (Cascella et al. 1991) and anorexia nervosa was found to give rise to reduced total brain volume that was reversible with increase in weight (Artmann et al. 1985; Enzmann and Lane 1977; Kohlmeyer et al. 1983). Because the technique uses ionising radiation and because of a number of other advantages of MRI, CT is no longer the research technique of choice in most psychiatric disorders. CT still has a place in clinical practice, though this is more limited as the availability of MRI machines has increased.

Magnetic resonance imaging

MRI has a complex mechanism of action that fundamentally depends on the *spin* of biologically abundant atomic nuclei with an uneven number of electrons. When a strong magnetic field is applied externally these nuclei align with the field, and once the nuclei are excited into a higher energy state by a burst of radio frequency, this energy is emitted as a radio wave and detected by the MRI scanner, a process known as *relaxation*. Depending on the radio frequency that is applied by the scanner, the relaxation is of type T1 or T2, and the resulting images are said to be either T1 weighted or T2 weighted. To demonstrate structural neuroanatomical features T1 weighted images are useful, as fluid appears dark and white matter is brighter in appearance than grey matter. However, in T2 weighted images the situation is reversed, with fluid appearing bright and grey matter brighter than white matter – such images are used to demonstrate states such as brain oedema. MRI is much safer for the subject than CT scanning as no potentially harmful ionising radiation is used in the process, although patients can find the experience in the MRI scanner extremely distressing, particularly if they suffer from claustrophobia. The cramped close environment and the long period that the subject must remain still make it hard for some patients to endure. This applies particularly to patients with ID, who may have a limited understanding of the need for the experience. Patients must be free of 'magnetisable' materials as the powerful magnets on which MR relies could cause displacement and disruption of vital anatomic structures. Extensive check-lists exist for this purpose. Examples of the research and clinical uses of MR techniques are given below.

Magnetic resonance spectroscopy (MRS)

MRS works on the principle that brain metabolites contain nuclei that have characteristic emission characteristics in particular chemical contexts. This technique enables brain metabolites to be quantified without direct access to brain matter, and their alteration monitored in certain pathological brain conditions. MRS is useful in situations where there is neuronal death – e.g., stroke, tumour, infections and demyelinating diseases. A marker of neuronal density, N-acetylaspartate (NAA) (an amino acid that occurs only in the membranes of neuronal cells), has been measured using MRS in a range of disorders leading to ID, including pervasive developmental disorders, Down syndrome and others (see below).

Functional magnetic resonance imaging (fMRI)

fMRI was developed in the early 1990s and the technology has moved on remarkably since these early days. It is a minimally invasive technique that allows extremely detailed image resolution, and provides an invaluable tool to investigate normal and abnormal brain function. fMRI has led to huge advances in psychiatric research, and is particularly useful in the field of pervasive developmental disorder and ID. It measures the small signal changes that relate to changes in the concentration of deoxyhaemoglobin in the blood. Since more metabolically active regions of the brain accumulate higher concentrations of deoxyhaemoglobin, so these areas are identified, and this allows the fMRI scanner to identify which region of the brain is active during a particular cognitive task.

Diffusion tensor magnetic resonance imaging (DT-MRI)

MRI has been further refined with advancing technology. It is now possible to analyse the volume and integrity of white matter tracts *in vivo* using DT-MRI tractography. This is a non-invasive neuroimaging technique designed to reconstruct three-dimensional trajectories of white matter tracts within the living brain (Catani et al. 2002) and probe the microstructural integrity of white matter in a wide range of conditions (Catani 2006). This technique can be combined with other sophisticated investigative techniques such as fractional anisotropy (FA) – an indirect measure of white matter spatial organisation and integrity (Beaulieu 2002). Fractional anisotropy quantifies the directionality of water diffusion on a scale from zero (when diffusion is totally random) to one (when water molecules are able to diffuse in one direction only) (Beaulieu 2002). These techniques have recently been used at the Institute of Psychiatry to visualise the white matter tracts of disorders such as Asperger's syndrome and criminal psychopathy.

Positron emission tomography (PET)

The images in PET are formed by the detection of photons by a system of photomultiplier tubes behind a collimator array – the photons are produced when positrons emitted from radio-labelled compounds administered into the body collide with local electrons. Various different radio-labelled compounds have been developed for use in PET – this makes the system extremely flexible and allows the imaging of various different aspects of brain morphology and function. PET can be used to gain information about brain receptor location and density, resting brain metabolism, and regional cerebral blood flow. In addition, PET has been used to measure changes in regional cerebral blood flow while the subject is performing a cognitive task. This technique can be used to investigate normal cognitive function, including cognitive function in those with ID.

NORMAL BRAIN DEVELOPMENT

To consider brain structure and function in neurodevelopmental disorders meaningfully, we must first have a basic understanding of normal brain development. Our understanding of normal brain development has been significantly advanced by the techniques described above. The first studies of the human brain were performed on post-mortem specimens, and it was found that the size of the brain quadruples in the first decade of life, and then gradually declines as the person ages further (Debakan and Sadowsky 1978). MRI studies have demonstrated the appearance of white matter tracts from one year of age, and also the continuation of the myelination process well into adolescence (e.g. Barkowich et al. 1988; Christophe et al. 1990; Holland et al. 1986), though the process peaks at around age 20 (Jernigan et al. 1991a; Pfefferbaum et al. 1994). The previously observed age-related loss of brain matter seems to be mainly accounted for by loss of grey matter (Pfefferbaum et al. 1994; Resnick et al. 2003), and this loss varies from region to region; for example, loss from the aging frontal lobes, less loss in temporal lobes and a relative sparing of parieto-occipital regions (Resnick et al. 2000; DeCarli et al. 1994; Murphy et al. 1992). The amount of cerebro-spinal fluid increases in the ageing brain (Jernigan et al. 1990, 1991a, 1991b; Pfefferbaum et al. 1994). Some MRI investigations have supported gender effects on age-related changes (e.g., Resnick et al. 2000) but these differences are not consistently demonstrated in other studies.

NEUROIMAGING: HELPING US UNDERSTAND NEURODEVELOPMENTAL DISORDERS

There follow some illustrative examples of ways in which neuroimaging techniques have been used to investigate conditions associated with specific or generalised ID.

Pervasive developmental disorders

Imaging studies of people suffering from autistic spectrum disorder have suggested an unusual increase in brain volume (e.g., Courchesne et al. 2001; Eliez and Reiss 2000). In addition, studies have commonly demonstrated changes in cerebellar pathology in people with autism – both cerebellar hypoplasia (Courchesne et al. 1988; Gafney et al. 1987; Hashimoto et al. 1995; Murakami et al. 1989) and an increase in cerebellar volume have been observed (Herbert et al. 2003; Sparks et al. 2002; Harden et al. 2001; Piven et al. 1997). Imaging studies have shown that the posterior regions of the corpus callosum are smaller in people with autism than controls, and this suggests a deficit in inter-hemispheric communication in autism (e.g. Saitoh et al. 1995; Egaas et al. 1995; Zilbovicius et al. 1995). Recently, some interesting work has been done using 'event-related' MRI to study facial emotion processing in Asperger's syndrome (AS) (Deeley et al. 2007). It was found that while subjects with AS and healthy controls both demonstrated an activation of facial perception areas (including fusiform and extrastriate cortices) to increasing intensities of fear and happiness, there was a marked hyporesponsiveness of these areas in the AS group compared to the controls (Deeley et al. 2007). This relative lack of brain activation in response to facial expressions may partly explain the social impairments of people suffering with AS.

Thus it is clear that people with pervasive developmental disorders demonstrate widespread abnormalities in brain development and inter-hemispheric connectivity. Though the exact aetiology of the disorders remains elusive, one could postulate that this widespread abnormality may underlie the cognitive and social deficits that are characteristic of the disorders.

Fragile X syndrome (FRAX)

If ID arises as an inherited disorder, then the commonest form of this is FRAX. FRAX is caused by an increase in the number of CGG triplet repeats in the fMR-1 gene on the X-chromosome. Individuals with FRAX experience varying degrees of developmental delay, and there are significant gender differences in the resulting cognitive phenotype. Most males who have a full mutation of FRAX suffer with a significant ID, usually presenting in the moderate or severe range (Kemper et al. 1986, 1988). The cognitive profile is less severe and more variable in females with FRAX than males (Freund and Reiss 1991; Kemper et al. 1986). MRI studies looking at individuals with FRAX have shown changes in the size of the cerebellar vermis, fourth ventricle, hippocampus and caudate volume that correlate closely to the percentage of active X chromosomes carrying the FRAX mutation (Reiss et al. 1995). It is known that increased phenotypic expression of FRAX is associated with a reduction in the amount of fragile X mental retardation protein (FMPR), and levels of this protein have been demonstrated by fMRI to be related to increased cortical activity during arithmetic (Rivera et al. 2002) and working memory tasks (Kwon et al. 2001). This suggests that there is a gene dosage dependent effect on the development of the brain.

Down syndrome (DS)

DS is associated with an extremely high prevalence of ID, age-related cognitive decline, and Alzheimer's disease (Haxby 1989; Shapiro et al. 1989), though the neurobiological basis for this remains unclear. An early CT scanning study examining the brains of young adults with DS reported a reduction in whole brain volume (Shapiro et al. 1989), and an early volumetric MRI study demonstrated a reduction in the volume of frontal cortex and cerebellum along with angulation of the brain stem (Kesslak et al. 1994). More recent studies in this extensively researched field include finding a loss of grey matter in the medial temporal lobe and corpus callosum in non-demented adults with DS. This finding may represent neuronal loss resulting from underlying but not yet clinically manifested Alzheimer's disease pathology (Teipel et al. 2004).

Velo-cardio-facial syndrome (VCFS)

VCFS is caused by a deletion at chromosome 22q11, and as the size of the deletion varies so do the manifestations of the disorder, both physically and mentally. VCFS is associated with ID (mild and borderline), psychosis (10–30%) and other mental illnesses (Pulver et al. 1994). Structural MRI has demonstrated decreased cerebellar and right temporal grey matter volumes in people with VCFS, along with increased grey matter volume in the left temporal lobes and part of the frontal lobes compared to controls (Van Amelsvoort et al. 2001). It has also been shown that children with VCFS have more pronounced deficits in white matter than grey matter volume (Eliez et al. 2000; Kates et al. 2001). Because the deletion in VCFS involves a number of genes that are hypothesised to be involved in the genesis of psychosis, the disorder provides an opportunity to explore the effects of the deleted regions on psychotic disorders, and there is currently considerable interest in this area.

BRAIN IMAGING IN CLINICAL PRACTICE

During early development, neuroimaging can be used to identify the consequences of traumatic brain injury associated with cerebral palsy resulting from perinatal CNS insults (such as smaller brain volume, dilated lateral ventricles and porencephalic cavities; Suvossa et al. 1990). In later life, about one-third of people with an ID will have a structural brain abnormality that can be detected by neuroimaging – this association becomes more pronounced as the ID becomes more severe, though the abnormalities are non-specific (Deb 1997; Van Karnebeek et al. 2005). If a person has a significant risk of developing progressive brain pathology later in life, such as a person with Down syndrome, there is a strong argument for a baseline MRI scan for potential future comparison. In other conditions associated with ID, or in 'idiopathic' ID, it can be argued that a baseline MRI scan is useful because it may enable developmental structural neuropathology to be differentiated from new pathology, should the clinical picture have changed.

Otherwise, the indications for scanning a person with ID are not dissimilar to those for scanning a person without ID; however, relative difficulty in establishing a person with ID's orientation status, difficulty in establishing the absence of an acute confusional state, and difficulty establishing a patient's thought contents may lower the threshold for use of neuroimaging. Indeed, careful investigation to rule out an underlying organic pathology is particularly crucial in those with an ID, as a person with ID may be less able to describe and articulate their 'psychiatric' symptoms, thus increasing the chance of missing organic aetiology. It could be argued that as ID becomes more severe, the threshold for neuroimaging should be reduced.

Changes in brain morphology that are consequent on a 'syndromal' cause of ID can often be studied, pooled together, and provide interesting insights into ID. However, in individual cases it is often impossible to identify specific changes in brain of sufficient magnitude for them to be useful diagnostically or in planning treatment. With very few exceptions (for example, the tubers of tuberose sclerosis), neuroimaging data derived from individual patients lacks the specificity to contribute to an understanding of the aetiology of a patient's difficulties. It remains to be seen if this picture will change.

BEHAVIOURAL GENETICS CLINIC

Neuroimaging is an integral part of the Maudsley's Behavioural Genetics Clinic (BGC), as both a research tool and a clinical assessment procedure. The clinic specialises in the diagnosis, in adults, of pervasive developmental disorders (the autistic spectrum), attention deficit hyperactivity disorders, and other mental disorders in which there is a clear behavioural phenotype. Neuroimaging is one means of investigating the endophenotypes that 'mediate' between the genotype (or environmental influence) and the behavioural manifestations of such disorders. Others include neuropsychological and quantitative psychiatric, physical and metabolic examinations. The clinic uses the latest technology to explore genotype/endophenotype/behavioural phenotype relations in order to better understand the aetiology of ID, and associated social and behavioural disorders. It is to be hoped that treatments will follow.

In cases of ID a genetic aetiology is common and is found in up to two-thirds of cases (Curry et al. 1997; for review see Basel-Vanagaite 2008). In clinic, alongside psychiatric, physical, neuropsychological and neuroimaging examinations, a patient is also offered karyotyping and other testing, if available, for genetic contributors to the relevant phenotype. We have a close relationship with our colleagues in the Clinical Genetics Clinic at Guy's Hospital, and this is often helpful in guiding our investigations. In addition the Guy's clinic provides us with the ability to refer patients on locally for family planning or other clinical genetic advice.

The BGC sees several new cases each week where the main referral question relates to the presence or absence of a pervasive developmental disorder. Of those people diagnosed with autism, about 3% have a maternally inherited chromosomal duplication in the Angelman syndrome/Prada-Willi syndrome region of 15q11–q13 (Basel-Vanagaite 2008), and a further 3–5% demonstrate other chromosomal abnormalities (Reddy 2005). It is thought that about 1% of cases of autism are caused by a microdeletion along with a reciprocal microduplication at 16p11.2 (Weiss et al. 2008). The BGC is involved in a wide range of basic science and clinical research projects aimed at understanding and treating pervasive developmental and other developmental disorders.

NECESSARY STEPS TO BETTER SERVICES

- Neuroimaging is a clinically valuable tool that with technological advances has become increasingly refined and ever more available to both patients and researchers.
- Neuroimaging provides a way for us to examine environmental and genetic factors in brain development and ageing.
- Neuroimaging is particularly useful in the field of ID where we often encounter morphometrically abnormal brains.
- Neuroimaging has added significantly to our understanding of developmental brain disorders and continues to do so.

REFERENCES

Artmann, H., Grau, H., Adelmann, M. and Schleiffer, R. (1985) Reversible and non-reversible enlargement of cerebral spinal fluid spaces in anorexia nervosa. *Neuroradiology*, 27, 304–312.

Barkowich, A.J., Kjos, B.O., Jackson, D.E. and Norman, D. (1988) Normal maturation of the neonatal and infant brain: MR imaging at 1.5T. *Neuroradiology*, 166, 173–180.

Basel-Vanagaite, L. (2008) Clinical approaches to genetic mental retardation. *Genetic Mental Retardation*, 10, 821–826.

Beaulieu, C. (2002) The basis of anisotropic water diffusion in the nervous system – a technical review. *NMR in Biomedicine*, 15, 435–455.

Cascella, N.G., Pearlson, G., Wong, D.F., Broussole, E., Nagoshi, C., Margolin, R.A. and London, E.D. (1991) Effects of substance abuse on ventricular and sulcal measures assessed by computerised tomography. *British Journal of Psychiatry*, 159, 217–221.

Catani, M. (2006) Diffusion tensor magnetic resonance imaging tractography in cognitive disorders. *Current Opinion in Neurology*, 19, 599–606.

Catani, M., Howard, R.J., Pajevic, S. and Jones, D.K. (2002) Virtual in vivo interactive dissection of white matter fasciculi in the human brain. *NeuroImage*, 17, 77–94.

Christophe, C., Muller, M.F., Baleriaux, D., Kahn, A., Pardon, A., Perlmutter, N. et al. (1990) Mapping of normal brain maturation in infants on phase-sensitive inversion-recovery images. *Neuroradiology*, 32, 173–178.

Chua, S.E. and McKenna, P.J. (1995) Schizophrenia – a brain disease? A critical review of structural and functional cerebral abnormality in the disorder. *British Journal of Psychiatry*, 166, 563–582.

Courchesne, E., Yeung-Courchesne, R., Press, G., Hussain, J.R. and Jernigan, T.L. (1988) Hypoplasia of cerebellar vermal lobules V1 and V11 in autism. *New England Journal of Medicine*, 318, 1349–1354.

Courchesne, E., Karns, C.M., Davis, H.R., Ziccardi, R., Carper, R.A., Tigue, Z.D. et al. (2001) Unusual brain growth patterns in early life in patients with autistic disorders. *Neurology*, 57, 245–254.

Curry, C.J., Stevenson, R.E., Aughton, D., Byrne, J., Carey, J.C., Cassidy, S. et al. (1997) Evaluation of mental retardation: Recommendations of a consensus conference: American College of Medical Genetics. *American Journal of Medical Genetics*, 72, 468–477.

Deb, S. (1997) Structural neuroimaging in learning disability. *British Journal of Psychiatry*, 171, 417–419.

Debakan, A.S. and Sadowsky, D. (1978) Changes in brain weights during the span of human life: Relation of brain weights to body heights and body weights. *Annals of Neurology*, 4, 345–356.

DeCarli, C.D., Murphy, D.G.M., Gillette, J.A., Haxby, J.V., Teichberg, D., Schapiro, M.B. and Horwitz, B. (1994) Lack of age-related differences in temporal lobe volume of very healthy adults. *American Journal of Neuroradiology*, 15, 689–696.

Deeley, Q., Daly, E.M., Surguladze, S., Page, L., Toal, F., Robertson, S. et al. (2007) An event related functional magnetic resonance imaging study of facial emotional processing in Asperger syndrome. *Biological Psychiatry*, 62, 207–217.

Egaas, B., Courchesne, E. and Saitoh, O. (1995) Reduced size of corpus callosum in autism. *Archives of Neurology*, 52, 794–801.

Eliez, S. and Reiss, A. (2000) Neuroimaging of childhood psychiatric disorders: A selective review. *Journal of Child Psychology and Psychiatry*, 41, 679–694.

Eliez, S., White, C., Schmitt, E., Menon, V. and Reiss, A.L. (2000) Children and adolescents with velocardialfacial syndrome: A volumetric study. *American Journal of Psychiatry*, 157, 409–415.

Enzmann, D.R. and Lane, B. (1977) Cranial computed tomography findings in anorexia nervosa. *Journal of Computer Assisted Tomography*, 1, 410–414.

Freund, L.S. and Reiss, A.L. (1991) Cognitive profiles associated with Fra (X) syndrome in males and females. *American Journal of Medical Genetics*, 38, 542–547.

Gafney, G.R., Tsai, L.Y., Kuperman, S. and Minchin, S. (1987) Cerebellar structure in autism. *American Journal of Diseases in Children*, 141, 1330–1332.

Harden, A.Y., Minshew, N.J., Mallikarjuhn, M. and Keveshan, M.S. (2001) Posterior fossa magnetic resonance imaging in autism. *Journal of American Child and Adolescent Psychiatry*, 40, 666–672.

Hashimoto, T., Tayama, M., Murakawa, K., Yoshimoto, T., Miyazaki, M., Harada, M. and Kuroda, Y. (1995) Development of the brainstem and cerebellum in autistic patients. *Journal of Autism and Developmental Disorders*, 25, 1–18.

Haxby, J.V. (1989) Neuropsychological evaluation of adults with Down syndrome: Patterns of selective impairment in non-demented old adults. *Journal of Mental Deficiency Research*, 33, 193–210.

Herbert, M.R., Ziegler, D.A., Deutsch, C.K., O'Brien, L.M., Lange, M., Bakardjiev, A. et al. (2003) Dissociations of cerebral cortex, subcortical and cerebral white matter volumes in autistic boys. *Brain*, 126, 1182–1192.

Holland, B.A., Haas, D.K., Norman, D., Brant-Zawadski, M. and Newton, T.H. (1986) MRI of normal brain maturation. *American Journal of Neuroradiology*, 7, 201–208.

Jernigan, T.L., Archibald, S.L., Berhow, M.T., Sowell, E.R., Foster, D.S. and Hesselink, J.R. (1991a) Cerebral structure on MRI, Part 1: Localization of age-related changes. *Biological Psychiatry*, 29, 55–67.

Jernigan, T.L., Press, G.A. and Hesselink, J.R. (1990) Methods for measuring brain morphologic features on magnetic resonance images: Validation and normal aging. *Archives of Neurology*, 47, 27–32.

Jernigan, T.L., Salmon, D., Butters, N. and Hesselink, J.R. (1991b) Cerebral structure on MRI, Part II: Specific changes in Alzheimer's and Huntington's diseases. *Biological Psychiatry*, 29, 68–81.

Kates, W.R., Burnette, C.P., Jabs, E.W., Rutberg, J., Murphy, A.M., Grades, M. et al. (2001) Regional cortical white matter reductions in velocardiofacial syndrome: A volumetric MRI analysis. *Society of Biological Psychiatry*, 49, 677–684.

Kemper, M.B., Hagerman, R.J., Ahmad, R.S. and Mariner, R. (1986) Cognitive profiles and the spectrum of clinical manifestations in heterozygous fragile-X females. *American Journal of Medical Genetics*, 23, 139–156.

Kemper, M.B., Hagerman, R.J. and Altshul-Stark, D. (1988) Cognitive profiles of boys with the fragile-X syndrome. *American Journal of Human Genetics*, 30, 191–200.

Kesslak, J.P., Nagata, B.S., Lott, M.D. and Nalcoiglu, O. (1994) Magnetic resonance imaging of brain age-related changes in the brains of individuals with Down's syndrome. *Neurology*, 44, 1039–1045.

Kohlmeyer, K., Lehmkuhl, G. and Poutska, F. (1983) Computed tomography of anorexia nervosa. *American Journal of Neuroradiology*, 4, 437–438.

Kwon, H., Menon, V., Eliez, S., Warsofsky, I.S., White, C.D., Dyer-Friedman, J. et al. (2001) Functional neuroanatomy of visuospatial working memory in fragile-X syndrome: Relation to behavioural and molecular measures. *American Journal of Psychiatry*, 158, 1040–1051.

Murakami, J., Courchesne, E., Press, G., Yeung-Courchesne, R. and Hesselink, J. (1989) Reduced cerebellar hemisphere size and its relationship to vermal hypoplasia in autism. *Archives of Neurology*, 46, 689–694.

Murphy, D.G.M., DeCarli, C.D., Schapiro, M.B., Rapoport, S.I. and Horowitz, B. (1992) Age-related differences in volumes of subcortical nuclei, brain matter, and cerebrospinal fluid in healthy men as measured with MRI. *Archives of Neurology*, 49, 839–849.

Pfefferbaum, A., Mathalon, D.H., Sullivan, E.V., Rawles, J.M., Zipursky, R.B. and Lim, K.O. (1994) A quantitative magnetic resonance imaging study of changes in brain morphology from infancy to late adulthood. *Archives of Neurology*, 51, 874–887.

Piven, J., Saliba, K., Baily, J. and Arndt, S. (1997) An MRI study of autism: The cerebellum revisited. *Neurology*, 49, 546–551.

Pulver, A.E., Nestadt, G., Goldberg, R., Shprintzen, R.J., Lamacz, M., Wolyniec, P.S. et al. (1994) Psychotic illness in patients diagnosed with velo-cardio-facial syndrome and their relatives. *Journal of Nervous and Mental Disease*, 182, 476–478.

Reddy, K.S. (2005) Cytogenetic abnormalities and fragile-X syndrome in autism spectrum disorder. *Medical Genetics*, 6, 3.

Reiss, A.L., Abrams, M.T., Greenlaw, R., Freund, L. and Denckla, M. (1995) Neuro-developmental effects of the FMR-1 full mutation in humans. *Nature Medicine*, 1, 159–167.

Resnick, S.M., Goldszal, A.F., Davatszikos, C., Golski, S., Kraut, M.A., Metter, E.J. et al. (2000) One year age changes in MRI brain volumes in older adults. *Cerebral Cortex*, 10, 464–472.

Resnick, S.M., Pham, D.L., Kraut, M.A., Zonderman, A.B. and Davastzikos, C. (2003) Longitudinal magnetic resonance imaging studies of older adults: A shrinking brain. *Neuropsychologica*, 23, 3259–3301.

Rivera, S.M., Menon, V., White, C.D., Glaser, B. and Reiss, A.L. (2002) Functional brain activation during arithmetic processing in females with fragile X syndrome is related to FMR1 protein expression. *Human Brain Mapping*, 16, 206–218.

Saitoh, O., Courchesne, E., Egaas, B., Lincoln, A.J. and Screibman, L. (1995) Cross-sectional area of the posterior hippocampus in autistic patients with cerebellar and corpus callosum abnormalities. *Neurology*, 45, 317–324.

Shapiro, M.B., Luxenberg, J., Kaye, J., Haxby, J.V., Friedland, R.P. and Rapoport, S.I. (1989) Serial quantitative CT analysis of brain morphometrics in adult Down syndrome at different ages. *Neurology*, 39, 1349–1353.

Sparks, B.F., Friedman, F.D., Shaw, D.W., Aylward, E.H., Echelard, B.S., Artru, A.A. et al. (2002) Brain structural abnormalities in young children with autism spectrum disorder. *Neurology*, 59, 184–192.

Suvossa, J., Seidl, Z. and Faber, J. (1990) Hemiparesis of cerebral palsy in relation to epilepsy and mental retardation. *Development and Child Neurology*, 32, 792–794.

Teipel, S.J., Alexander, G.E., Schapiro, M.B., Möller, H.J., Rapoport, S.I. and Hampel, H. (2004) Age-related cortical grey matter reductions in non-demented Down's syndrome adults determined by MRI with voxel-based morphometry. *Brain*, 127, 811–824.

Van Amelsvoort, T., Daly, E., Robertson, D., Suckling, J., Ng, V., Critchley, H. et al. (2001) Structural brain abnormalities associated with deletion at chromosome 22q11: Quantitative neuroimaging study of adults with velo-cardio-facial syndrome. *British Journal of Psychiatry*, 178, 412–419.

Van Karnebeek, C.D., Jansweijer, M.C., Leenders, A.G., Offringa, M. and Hennekam, R.C. (2005) Diagnostic investigations in individuals with mental retardation: A systemic literature review of their usefulness. *European Journal of Human Genetics*, 13, 6–25.

Weiss, L.A., Shen, Y., Korn, J.M., Arking, D.E., Miller, D.T., Fossdal, R. et al. (2008) Association between microdeletion and microduplication at 16p11.2 and autism. *New England Journal of Medicine*, 358, 667–675.

Zilbovicius, M., Garreau, B., Samson, Y., Remy, P., Barthelemy, C., Syrota, A. and Lelord, G. (1995) Delayed maturation of the frontal cortex in childhood autism. *American Journal of Psychiatry*, 152, 248–252.

CHAPTER SEVEN

The association between psychopathology and intellectual disability

Max Pickard and Titi Akinsola

INTRODUCTION

Our understanding of psychopathology in people with intellectual disability (ID) is still far from complete, perhaps in part due to both conceptual and pragmatic difficulties in research. Nonetheless, immense strides have been taken in the past century, and the pace of understanding has quickened significantly over the past few decades.

The acceptance that ID is separate from mental illness led to a misconception that ID and mental illness could not occur simultaneously. The next conceptual hurdle was the understanding that, while separate entities, ID and mental illness could coexist. Indeed, evidence now suggests that the level of psychopathology in people with ID is at least as high, if not higher, than in the generic population (e.g. Bouras et al. 2004, Doody et al. 1998).

We are now at a stage where we are slowly building a more robust picture of how mental illness and ID interact. The challenges are significant; ID is highly heterogeneous by nature, we have major confounders with our evolving understanding of autistic spectrum disorder and neuropsychiatric conditions such as epilepsy and attention deficit disorder. Our increasing understanding of genotypes, phenotypes, personality, behaviour and even intelligence strains the demarcation of what 'mental illness', 'ID', and 'challenging behaviour' are. Nevertheless, despite these problems, we must continue to evolve our understanding of psychopathology and use the evidence as building blocks in this process.

The Estia centre has, over the course of its existence, produced a number of important studies on psychopathology. It has attempted to integrate research with training, service development, and clinical practice in a manner that is mutually beneficial. Epidemiological studies have informed service delivery decisions and development, and training, which in turn lead to outcome and evaluation studies, and further refinement of service delivery and clinical practice. This chapter will highlight the important research done on psychopathology and the implications this has for services.

ASSESSMENT OF PSYCHOPATHOLOGY

One of the building blocks of understanding is the process of assessing when psychopathology is present. Costello and Bouras (2006) review the assessment of psychopathology in people with ID. They draw attention to the problems: standardised rating scales often used in the generic population may be inappropriate when applied to the highly heterogeneous ID population, the increasing reliance on third-party reports as level of ID increases. However, they also note that the increased drive towards robust evidence-based practice in treating/assessing psychopathology in people with ID has led to development of specialised rating scales in this population.

With the development of tailored rating scales, not only will our understanding of the epidemiology of psychopathology increase, but so will our understanding of treatment. To evaluate any treatment requires measurement of psychopathology.

Services should consider carefully how to locate hidden mental health problems within the population. On one hand, intrusiveness is not to be condoned. On the other, mental health services should not be exclusively for those that present with challenging behaviour or crisis. The key may lie in ensuring that ground-level/front-line staff have some experience and training in basic mental health issues and hence can be alert to the quietly depressed, uncomplaining individual, or the isolating, irritable individual who may be in a prodromal stage of a psychotic illness. The use of easily administered screening tools may assist services. See Chapter 4 for further discussion.

Epidemiological studies of psychopathology in people with ID

The presence of psychopathology in ID may have many causes: genetic, organic, psychosocial, and so on. The highly heterogeneous nature of the ID population makes disentanglement particularly challenging.

Cowley et al. (2004) retrospectively analysed a large sample of referred cases (752). Psychopathology was associated with older age, mild ID (as opposed to more severe), and referral from generic mental health services.

People who had been admitted under the Mental Health Act were four times as likely to have a diagnosis of schizophrenia. The authors point out that the relatively low level of psychiatric diagnosis (half that of the mild and moderate group) in people with severe ID may be due to unrecognised psychiatric disorder. They also noted that people with mild ID were much more likely (47 times) to have a diagnosis of personality disorder than those with moderate and severe ID, perhaps indicating that the diagnosis of personality disorder is not a pragmatic one for more severely disabled individuals. This study highlights the need for mental health services to provide adequately for people with mild ID and psychiatric diagnosis (ensuring good care pathways so that individuals are not lost between generic mental health and specialist ID mental health services), and also reminds us that vigilance is needed to detect psychopathology in individuals with more severe ID.

PSYCHOPATHOLOGY AND SCHIZOPHRENIA

In a review of literature, Turner (1989) reports a point prevalence of 3% for schizophrenia in ID, a figure three times that of the general population. Schizophrenia itself is associated with premorbid cognitive impairments (Russell et al. 1997, Niemi et al. 2003).

Moving on from purely epidemiological studies on incidence rates, Doody et al. (1998) compared three groups of individuals: with schizophrenia, with ID, and with both schizophrenia and ID. They found that the comorbid group (both schizophrenia and ID) had more negative symptoms, soft neurological signs, epilepsy, and received more community support than those with just schizophrenia.

Bouras et al. (2004) studied schizophrenia spectrum disorders in people with and without mild ID. They found that people with both schizophrenia spectrum disorders and comorbid ID were more debilitated, had increased observable psychopathology, were more likely to have an additional diagnosis of epilepsy and had more negative symptoms of the illness than the comparison group without ID. They found no difference in behavioural problems. Interestingly, a robust finding was that those without ID were more likely to have had a life stressor recently. The study notes some confounders; in particular, the population without ID had a higher proportion of men. Despite this, the study gives strong weight to the argument that the comorbidity of schizophrenia and ID is a particularly disabling and challenging condition.

Johnstone et al. (2007) looked into whether it would be possible to identify people with ID 'at risk' of developing a future psychotic illness. Using a sample of 394 (of whom, given the prevalence of 3% of schizophrenia, around 12 would be expected to develop the illness) who received a variety of standardised tests, the authors concluded that there was a neuropsychological and psychopathological profile that was consistent with an extended phenotype of schizophrenia; a group that may be at enhanced liability to develop the full-blown illness. This study might indicate that future research and mental health services could investigate identification and targeting of health resources to people at particular risk of developing this serious illness. It is perhaps too early to speculate whether this may actually divert an individual away from developing an illness, or improve long-term prognosis, but this is an avenue that should be explored with a degree of cautious optimism.

The UK700 study was a large UK-based randomised controlled trial comparing standard and intensive case management in the treatment of patients with psychosis (UK700 Group 1999). Mild ID (IQ range 51–70) on psychometric testing was found in 8% of the sample. The authors suggest that adult mental health services should be aware of the high level of cognitive impairment (including borderline intellectual functioning) in service users with schizophrenia, and argue for closer links between adult mental health services and specialist ID services.

This evidence strongly suggests not only that people with ID are more at risk of developing schizophrenia, but that should they do so, the impairments are worse and the prognosis less good. For health services, this translates to greater needs and challenges. Far from considering mental health services for people with ID as a 'Cinderella' service, the evidence indicates a need for higher quality and better resourced mental health and social care services.

PSYCHOPATHOLOGY AND AFFECTIVE DISORDER

Affective disorder is not uncommon in the ID population. Richards (2001) reported increased risk of affective disorders in people with mild ID, even after controlling for social and material disadvantages and medical conditions. Collacott et al. (1992) described a higher prevalence of depression in adults with Down syndrome than in other causes of ID.

Smiley (2005) reported for bipolar disorder a lifetime prevalence rate of 1.5% in ID compared to 1% in the general population. Deb and Hunter (1991) reported cyclical changes in behaviour and mood in 4% of people with ID. In addition to changes in typical affective, biological and motor activities, frequent atypical symptoms have been suggested by Turner (1989), including disturbed, aggressive behaviour, bizarre rituals and 'hysterical' behaviour. They explained that this might be in the context of hallucinations and persecutory feelings, leading to fear and outbursts particularly among people with moderate to severe ID.

SPECIFIC FACTORS ASSOCIATED WITH PSYCHOPATHOLOGY IN ID

Life events

When considering improving global population mental health, the association between potentially toxic life events and developing psychopathology is clearly of interest. This is no less, and possibly more, relevant for people with ID who often are subjected to significant psychosocial disadvantage. Tsakanikos et al. (2006a) looked at exposure to life events and associated clinical psychopathology in people with ID. This was a retrospective study on data collected as part of service delivery (not data collected for the purpose of research), but nevertheless some interesting findings emerged. Logistic regression showed that a single exposure to life events was associated with schizophrenia, personality disorder, and depression (as well as female gender). Exposure to multiple life events was associated with personality disorder, depression and adjustment reaction. While causality cannot be presumed, this research lends considerable weight to the hypothesis that adverse life events are powerfully intertwined with psychopathology. It is interesting to note that one of the most frequent life events was 'move of house/residence'.

This research suggests that either such moves have a harmful effect on an individual's mental health, or poor mental health increases the chances of such moves (or both). In either case the findings should give cause for mental health and social services to reflect on their local strategy for residential provision and support.

Autism

Autistic spectrum disorder is strongly associated with ID (Fonbonne 1999). All ID services must be very familiar with the range of problems and service requirements that go hand in hand with autism. However, people with autism and ID may have additional mental health needs, adding another layer of complexity to an already complex presentation. While people with autism and ID could present with most mental health problems (the issues of personality disorder and obsessive compulsive disorder being particularly controversial for people with autism, a subject out of the scope of this monograph), it is important to know what particular mental health needs are associated with autism.

Tsakanikos et al. (2006c) examined psychiatric comorbidity in 752 adults with ID: 147 with comorbid autism, 605 without. All had been referred to specialist mental heath services in southeast London. The study indicated that people referred were more likely to receive a psychiatric diagnosis (excluding autism) if they also had comorbid autism. However, a diagnosis of personality disorder was less likely. The authors note that in the course of the study, they found that examples of old diagnoses of 'schizophrenia spectrum' and 'personality disorder' were often misdiagnoses of autistic spectrum disorder.

While further research is needed before confidently planning resources to meet the needs of the 'triple diagnosis' group; that of ID, mental illness, and autistic spectrum disorder, it is clear that this group is particularly challenging and complex. One difficulty that may arise in service delivery is that while social and health care services (particularly residential or inpatient ones) may be designed for the needs of people with either mental illness or autistic spectrum disorder (in conjunction with ID), people with all three diagnoses do not neatly fit into one or the other. A challenge for services is to provide services that are able to meet the needs of all three concurrent diagnoses, i.e. to fit services around individuals, rather than attempt to shoehorn such complex problems into one service or another.

Gender

The differences in diagnoses of psychopathology between men and women are well recognised and known (e.g. American Psychiatric Association 1994). However, most research has been performed without attending to people with ID. More recent studies have suggested that affective disorders may be more common in women with ID (e.g. Lunsky 2003) than in the general population.

Tsakanikos et al. (2006b) examined 590 referrals to a specialist Mental Health in ID Service in SE London: half men, half women. They found that men were diagnosed with personality disorder more than women. Women were diagnosed with dementia and adjustment reaction more commonly. It is interesting to note the discrepancy in pathway to the service; women were more likely to be referred through primary care, while men were more likely to be referred through generic mental health services. Although highly speculative, this might tentatively suggest that men are less likely to seek help for, or complain of, mental health problems.

There needs to be a better understanding of the effect gender has on prevalence, presentation, treatment and prognosis of mental health problems in people with ID, as this would help map out specialist services. The evidence starts to suggest, as one would suspect, that the effect of gender is broadly similar to that in the general population. There are future questions that services need to address, such as the need for gender-specific settings or treatment groups, how to address gender-specific broad mental health issues (self-esteem, sexual functioning, etc.), and how to ensure good publicity for services, destigmatisation of mental illness, and good pathway to primary and specialist health services for mental health problems for both men and women.

THE RELATIONSHIP BETWEEN PSYCHOPATHOLOGY AND BEHAVIOUR

Clinical assessment of psychopathology in mental health services should come from a multitude of sources. Often, the most useful source of information is the patient's verbal description of their inner mental state. However, as an individual's level of ID increases, the ability to communicate this verbally will fall. Initially, this will pose more challenges for eliciting subtle signs such as pseudohallucinations, as described by Pickard and Paschos (2005), but with increasing level of disability this mode of eliciting psychopathology becomes less valid (see also Chapter 4).

Instead, increasing attention and weight must be given to non-verbal communication and direct observation of behaviour. The relationship between behaviour (particularly 'challenging behaviour') and psychopathology is complex. However, it is reasonable to suppose that much psychopathology is detected by unusual behaviour, and much unusual behaviour is underpinned by psychopathology.

Hemmings et al. (2006) examined the relationship between behaviour (specifically, challenging behaviour) and mental health symptoms in a cross-sectional survey of 214 clients. While acknowledging the perennial difficulty of defining what exactly 'challenging behaviour' or 'problem behaviour' is, the study found an association of self-injurious and (to a lesser extent) aggressive behaviour with affective type symptoms. While autism is not always considered a mental illness, the study found that screaming and destructiveness were associated more with autistic spectrum problems as opposed to conventional psychiatric symptoms. The study does comment that causality is not proven; and the question of whether mental ill health causes challenging behaviour or challenging behaviour causes poor mental health is not as straightforward as it may initially appear. For instance, challenging behaviour can lead to isolation, bullying, and breakdown of many protective factors that sustain good mental health.

While more research is needed to elucidate the epidemiology and management of coexisting challenging behaviour and mental illness, services should carefully consider how to align themselves. The distinction between challenging behaviour and mental illness is not well demarcated. It is reasonable to suppose that there are, conceptually, three groups: challenging behaviour without significant mental illness (which requires a predominantly behavioural–environmental led approach), mental illness without significant challenging behaviour (which requires a predominantly bio-psycho-social assessment and treatment approach), and both challenging behaviour and significant mental illness (which often requires both approaches in an integrated, well-planned manner). Care must be given when stating that an individual's challenging behaviour is secondary to the mental illness, or indeed that an individual's mental illness is secondary to challenging behaviour; while this may indeed be true, such declarations can lead to individuals being deprived of treatment modalities.

PSYCHOPATHOLOGY AND PHARMACOTHERAPY

Indications for psychotropic medication in people with ID bear similarities to those in the general population, including affective, anxiety and psychotic disorders. Analysis of predictors of psychotropic medication receipt in people with ID suggest that while the receipt of antidepressants is predicted by symptoms of mental ill health, the receipt of both antipsychotics and hypnotic/anxiolytics is predicted by variables related to challenging behaviour for control of disruptive or aggressive behaviors (Robertson et al. 2000). A clinical naturalistic study in people with ID also suggested that olanzapine tended to be prescribed mostly for psychotic disorders, whereas risperidone was prescribed mostly for people with behavioural disturbance associated with a psychiatric diagnosis and/or behavioural disturbance associated with pervasive developmental disorder (Bokszanska et al. 2003).

The use of antipsychotic medication for people with ID is far in excess of the 4–6% (Deb and Fraser 1994; Cooper et al. 2007) expected prevalence of psychosis. The prescription rate of antipsychotic medication has been variously reported as between 10 and 50%: 25–50% for residents in NHS hospitals, 20–50% in community-based services and 10% for people living with natural or substituted families (Deb and Fraser 1994; Bradford 1994). Challenging behaviour is a common reason for referral to specialist ID service. It has been suggested that challenging behavior may play a key role in determining receipt of antipsychotic medication (Molyneux et al. 2000; Wressell et al. 1990). This was explored in an article by Tsakanikos et al. (2006c). A significantly larger proportion of people with pervasive developmental disorder displayed challenging problems such as aggressiveness, destructiveness, pestering others, self-injurious behaviour, screaming, temper tantrums and verbal abuse. They were more likely than matched controls to receive psychotropic medications in general and antipsychotics in particular. It also suggested that physical aggression and problems such as pestering staff independently predicted the use of antipsychotics.

There is limited robust research evidence for the effectiveness of antipsychotics in managing challenging behaviours in people with ID. Horrigan (1997) reported substantial improvement in young adult patients (small number: 11, mean age 18.3 years) with aggression, self-injurious behaviour, explosivity and poor sleep hygiene on risperidone, modal dose of 0.5 mg twice a day. In a double-blind randomised control trial comparing risperidone to placebo for treatment in autistic disorder accompanied by severe tantrums, aggression or self-injurious behaviour in 5–17 year olds, treatment with risperidone (dose 0.5–3.5 mg/day) resulted in almost 60% reduction in the irritability score, in comparison to 14.1% decrease with placebo (McCracken et al. 2002). In an older population (mean age 28.1 years, sample size 31), in a double-blind, placebo-controlled study, in autistic disorder, risperidone was found superior to placebo in reducing repetitive behaviour, aggression, irritability and overall behavioural symptoms of autism (McDougle 1998). A systematic review of randomised controlled trials for effectiveness of antipsychotic medication for challenging behaviour in people with ID concluded that there was a lack of trial-based evidence of the effectiveness or ineffectiveness of antipsychotic medication for adults with ID and challenging behaviour (Brylewski and Duggan 1999, 2007).

Most recently, the NACHBID (Neuroleptics for Aggressive Challenging Behaviour in Intellectual Disability) clinical trial compared the effectiveness of haloperidol, risperidone and placebo in reduction of aggression in people with ID (Tyrer et al. 2008). Patients with a clinical diagnosis of psychosis were excluded from the study. The Modified Overt Aggression Scale (MOAS) at baseline, 4, 12, and 26 weeks was used to assess the primary outcome of aggressive behaviour. Secondary outcome measures included aberrant behaviour, quality of life, adverse drug effects, carer uplift and burden, and total costs. A total of 86 patients, the majority of whom had mild to moderate ID, were randomly assigned to receive placebo ($n = 29$), risperidone ($n = 29$), or haloperidol ($n = 28$). The mean daily dose of risperidone was initially 1.07 mg and increased to 1.78 mg; that of haloperidol was initially 2.54 mg and increased to 2.94 mg. Rescue medication lorazepam was utilised in the trial. Results of the study revealed a reduction in aggression with all three treatment arms after four weeks; however, the placebo group had the greatest response (median decrease in MOAS score = 9 (95% CI: 5 to 14); a 79% reduction from baseline). This compared to a 58% reduction from baseline for risperidone (MOAS decrease = 7 (95% CI: 4 to 14)) and a 65% reduction from baseline for haloperidol (MOAS decrease = 6.5 (95% CI: 5 to 14)). In addition, patients given placebo showed no evidence of a significantly worse response at any time point during the study than those who were assigned to either of the antipsychotic drugs. All secondary outcome measures showed no differences between any of the treatment arms. The study limitation included being underpowered as the planned target sample was 144 while the study size was 86. The study concluded that there is no evidence that either risperidone or haloperidol, given in conventionally low doses, offers any advantages over placebo in treatment of aggressive challenging behaviour in ID.

It is suggested that placebo is more cost-effective than the other two treatments over a six-month period, in terms of total costs. This should not be interpreted as an indication that antipsychotic medications have no place in the treatment of some aspects of behaviour problems in people with ID.

THE IMPORTANCE OF PSYCHOPATHOLOGY AND FURTHER RESEARCH

Aside from the direct benefits of detecting and thus treating psychopathology in people with ID, it is important to continue refining our knowledge in this field. As discussed, the assessment of psychopathology in people with ID is complicated, and hence prone to difficulties.

One problem might be seeing 'mirages', i.e. seeing psychopathology that is not actually present. This is concerning, as needless (at best) or harmful (at worst) treatment may result. In addition, it may distract services from providing the non-health-based support that is needed, while waiting for a 'recovery' or 'improvement' from a non-existent illness, which never actually arises.

The other problem is equally concerning: that of missing the true cause of problems, or failing to notice the invisible psychopathology that is behind the manifest problem. In such cases, one is failing to treat the potentially treatable. Potentially avoidable personal suffering and limitations in social choices may be the consequence.

Progress has been made with progressively more accurate epidemiological studies (Cooper et al. 2007). We should be careful to avoid an unfounded belief that specific psychopathologies are non-existent, exceptionally rare, or indeed 'normal' and to be expected. We can become more accurate at identifying risk factors for developing psychopathology, both increasing our diagnostic accuracy and potentially addressing broad psychosocial interventions to help reduce psychopathology.

Future research directions should consider:

- how best to use resources in terms of service delivery, such as the impact of high-intensity community services on long-term prognosis, targeting resources on 'at risk' populations to divert from developing serious mental illness
- identification of needs for specialist mental health services in people with ID (such as personality disorder services, drug and alcohol services, forensic services, psychiatric intensive care services), and how to deliver these in conjunction with non-ID mental health services
- the psychopathology and prognosis of mental health problems in people with both autistic spectrum disorders and major mental illness

(such as schizophrenia), including analysis of how degree of autistic spectrum problems interacts with mental health

- effect of gender on prevalence of mental health issues, and how gender may influence care pathways, prognosis, and relevant protective and predisposing factors such as self-esteem, social roles, relationships, and gender identity
- clarification of impact of mental illness on behaviour, considering causality and the effect on behaviour of treating mental illness.

NECESSARY STEPS TO BETTER SERVICES

- Adequate social care and mental health resources to work intensively with people with ID and severe mental illness (such as schizophrenia).
- A full spectrum of resources to fit service user needs, rather than service users fitting into resources; access to a range of in-patient and out-patient services including other specialist mental health services.
- Effective high-intensity community resources directed at those developing, or at high risk of developing, serious mental health problems.
- Specialist mental health and social service resources (including training and expertise) for people with both comorbid psychiatric illness and autistic spectrum disorder.
- Ensuring good publicity of services, distigmatisation of mental illness, and promoting broad good mental health in the community in large. Including addressing race, cultural, and gender issues.
- Clear care pathways and integrated service delivery between 'challenging behaviour' services and 'mental health' services, accepting that while the treatment modalities may differ, the two concepts are not easy to demarcate.

REFERENCES

American Psychiatric Association (1994) *Diagnostic and Statistical Manual of Mental Disorders* (4th ed.). Washington, DC: American Psychiatric Association.

Bokszkanska, A., Graham, M., Vanstraelen, M., Holt, G., Bouras, N. and Taylor, D. (2003) Risperidone and olanzapine in adults with intellectual disability: A clinical naturalistic study. *International Clinical Psychopharmacology*, 18, 285–291.

Bouras, N., Martin, G., Leese, M., Vanstraelen, M., Holt, G., Thomas, C. et al. (2004) Schizophrenia-spectrum psychoses in people with and without intellectual disability. *Journal of Intellectual Disability Research*, 48 (6), 548–555.

Bradford, D. (1994) A study of the prescribing for people with learning disabilities living in the community and in National Health Service care. *Journal of Intellectual Disability Research*, 38, 577–586.

Brylewski, J. and Duggan, L. (1999) Antipsychotic medication for challenging behaviour in people with intellectual disability: A systematic review of randomised controlled trials. *Journal of Intellectual Disability Research*, 43, 360–371.

Brylewski, J. and Duggan, L. (2007) Antipsychotic medication for challenging behaviour in people with intellectual disability: A systematic review of randomised controlled trials. *Cochrane Database of Systematic Reviews*, 3, CD000377.

Collacott, R.A., Cooper, S.A. and McGrother, C. (1992) Differential rates of psychiatric disorders in adults with Down's syndrome compared with other mentally handicapped adults. *British Journal of Psychiatry*, 161, 671–674.

Cooper, S.A., Smiley, E., Morrison, J., Williamson, A. and Allan, L. (2007) Mental ill-health in adults with intellectual disabilities: Prevalence and associated factors. *British Journal of Psychiatry*, 190, 27–35.

Costello, H. and Bouras, N. (2006) Assessment of mental health problems in people with intellectual disabilities. *Israel Journal of Psychiatry and Related Sciences*, 43 (4), 241–251.

Cowley, A., Holt, G., Bouras, N., Sturmey, P., Newton, J.T. and Costello, H. (2004) Descriptive psychopathology in people with mental retardation. *Journal of Nervous and Mental Disease*, 192 (3), 232–237.

Deb, S. and Fraser, W. (1994) The use of psychotropic medication in people with learning disability: Towards rational prescribing. *Human Psychopharmacology*, 9, 259–272.

Deb, S. and Hunter, D. (1991) Psychopathology of people with mental handicap and epilepsy: Psychiatric illness. *British Journal of Psychiatry*, 159, 826–830.

Doody, G.A., Johnstone, E.C., Sanderson, T.L., Owens, D.G. and Muir, W.J. (1998) 'Pfropfschizophrenie' revisited. Schizophrenia in people with mild learning disability. *British Journal of Psychiatry*, 173 (8), 145–153.

Fonbonne, E. (1999) The epidemiology of autism: A review. *Psychological Medicine*, 29, 769–786.

Hemmings, C.P., Gravestock, S., Pickard, M. and Bouras, N. (2006) Psychiatric symptoms and problem behaviours in people with intellectual disabilities. *Journal of Intellectual Disability Research*, 50 (4), 269–276.

Horrigan, J.P. (1997) Risperidone and explosive aggressive autism. *Journal of Autism and Developmental Disorders*, 27 (3), 313–323.

Johnstone, E.C., Owens, D.G.C., Hoare, P., Gaur, S., Spencer, M.D. et al. (2007) Schizotypal cognitions as a predictor of psychopathology in adolescents with mild intellectual impairment. *British Journal of Psychiatry*, 191, 484–492.

Kraeplin, E. (1919) *Dementia Praecox and Paraphrenia*. Edinburgh, UK: Livingstone (pp. 275–276).

Lunsky, Y. (2003) Depressive symptoms in intellectual disability: Does gender play a role? *Journal of Intellectual Disability Research*, 47, 417–427.

Martorell, A. and Tsakanikos, E. (2008) Traumatic experiences and life events in people with intellectual disability. *Current Opinion in Psychiatry*, 21 (5), 445–448.

McCracken, J.T., McGough, J. and Shah, B. (2002) Risperidone in children with autism and serious behavioural problems. *New England Journal of Medicine*, 347 (5), 314–321.

McDougle, C.J. (1998) A double blind, placebo-controlled study of risperidone in adults with autistic disorder and other pervasive developmental disorders. *Archives of General Psychiatry*, 55, 633–641.

Molyneaux, P., Emerson, E. and Cane, A. (2000) Prescription of psychotropic medication to people with intellectual disabilities in primary health care settings. *Journal of Applied Research in Intellectual Disabilities*, 12, 46–57.

Niemi, L.T., Suvisaari, J.M., Tuulio-Henriksson, A. and Lönnqvist, J.K. (2003) Childhood developmental abnormalities in schizophrenia: Evidence from high-risk studies. *Schizophrenia Research*, 60, 239–258.

Pickard, M. and Paschos, D. (2005) Pseudohallucinations in people with intellectual disabilities: Two case reports. *Mental Health Aspects of Developmental Disability*, 8, 91–93.

Richards, M. (2001), Long term affective disorder in people with learning disability. *British Journal of Psychiatry*, 179, 523–527.

Robertson, J., Emerson, E., Gregory, N., Hatton, C., Kessissoglu, S. and Hallam, A. (2000) Receipt of psychotropic medication by people with intellectual disability in residential settings. *Journal of Intellectual Disability Research*, 44, 666–676.

Russell, A.S., Munro, J.C., Jones, P.B., Hemsley, D.R. and Murray, R.M. (1997) Schizophrenia and the myth of intellectual decline. *American Journal of Psychiatry*, 154, 635–639.

Smiley, E. (2005) Epidemiology of mental health problems in adults with learning disability: An update. *Advances in Psychiatric Treatment*, 11, 214–222.

Tsakanikos, E., Bouras, N., Costello, H. and Holt, G. (2006a) Multiple exposure to life events and clinical psychopathology in adults with intellectual disability. *Journal of Social Psychiatry and Psychiatric Epidemiology*, 42 (1), 24–28.

Tsakanikos, E., Costello, H., Holt, G., Bouras, N., Sturmey, P. and Newton, T. (2006c) Psychopathology in adults with autism and intellectual disability. *Journal of Autism and Developmental Disorders*, 36, 1123–1129.

Tsakanikos, E., Bouras, N., Sturmey, P. and Holt, G. (2006b) Psychiatric co-morbidity and gender differences in intellectual disability. *Journal of Intellectual Disability Research*, 50 (8), 582–587.

Turner, T.H. (1989) Schizophrenia and mental handicap: An historical review, with implications for further research. *Psychological Medicine*, 19 (2), 301–314.

Tyrer, P., Oliver-Africano, P.C., Ahmed, Z., Bouras, N., Cooray, S., Deb, S. et al. (2008) Risperidone, haloperidol and placebo in the treatment of aggressive challenging behaviour in patients with intellectual disability: A randomised controlled trial. *Lancet*, 371, 57–63.

UK700 Group (1999) Comparison of intensive and standard case management for patients with psychosis: Rationale of the trial. *British Journal of Psychiatry*, 174, 74–78.

Wressell, S.E., Tyrer, S.P. and Barney, T.P. (1990) Reduction in antipsychotic drug dosage in mentally handicapped patients: A hospital study. *British Journal of Psychiatry*, 157, 101–106.

PART III

Training as an integrated component of service delivery

Training professionals, family carers and support staff to work effectively with people with intellectual disability and mental health problems

Helen Costello, Steve Hardy, Elias Tsakanikos and Jane McCarthy

INTRODUCTION

There is very little research evidence that examines the effectiveness of training professionals and carers in the provision of services to people with intellectual disability (ID) and mental health problems. Although training is essential for effective service provision, the need for specific training on mental health in relation to people with ID has only been recognised in recent years. Currently such training is only a formal requirement for psychiatrists in the UK. This recognition is the first step in the process to develop training materials and to evaluate and refine them on the basis of the resulting evidence. This chapter reflects on where we are in this process. Although training materials have been developed to support effective service developments, these as yet have not been tested and refined through evaluation within large-scale controlled studies. Consequently this chapter begins by looking at the training currently developed and why it is especially important in the provision of effective mental health services to individuals with ID. Training initiatives for mental health professionals, family carers and support staff are outlined and the evidence available about the outcomes of staff training is reviewed. Finally, a series of recommendations are made for the delivery of training in respect to infrastructure, training materials and good practice dissemination.

THE ROLE OF TRAINING IN DEVELOPING
EFFECTIVE SERVICES

Although the precise nature of training in mental health and ID will vary across different professional groups, training performs a number of common functions in respect of developing effective services. Mental health problems among people with ID often manifest in atypical ways, they may coexist with various developmental disorders and this may result in highly complex clinical presentations. As many people with ID have impaired communication and are unable to describe subjective symptoms, standardised criteria for diagnosing mental health problems and traditional treatment methods may be compromised. On a fundamental level, therefore, training in mental health and ID is required by professionals to provide special skills in relation to diagnosis, treatment and support. Such training helps to familiarise professionals with the unique circumstances in which individuals with ID and mental health problems live and to raise awareness of the distinct problems they face. Training is also useful in disseminating the latest research evidence and ensuring best practice. The formal inclusion of this topic on the training curricula of all mental health professionals would help to ensure that once people have been identified as having a mental health problem, they receive the best treatment possible in accordance with unified standards, irrespective of their location.

Uneven service provision, together with diversity in service models, implies that practitioners must be equipped to work within a variety of settings alongside a broad range of professionals and carers. An ability to work effectively within the context of varying, possibly conflicting, perspectives, beliefs and interpretations is also vital. Special training in mental health issues provides a common language and framework for understanding, describing and discussing mental health problems. For example, mental health professionals play a key role in helping managers in residential services to adequately support individuals with ID and mental health problems in the community. They advise managers regarding the nature and quality of services provided and the appropriate skills required by staff. This requires careful collaboration and negotiation between the commissioners paying for services, the managers providing services and the professional specialists advising on the support people need to ensure that advice is both practicable and acted upon. Minimising potential discrepancies and gaps between the various professionals and staff involved in this process is critical in ensuring the success of complex care packages. In the absence of common knowledge, shared expertise and consistent specialist support, staff struggle alone and are vulnerable to poor morale and injury while service users are exposed to bad care practices and potential abuse (Department of Health 2007). This may lead to crises, placement breakdowns, reinstitutionalisation and the silting-up of special-ised services.

The formal recognition of mental health and ID and the availability of a comprehensive training structure is an important step in improving recruit-ment and retention. For example, Graham et al. (2004) reported that many trainee psychiatrists in ID felt unskilled and experienced feelings of impo-tence, hopelessness, and disempowerment. In addition, they felt alienated, both from the individuals with ID and from other professionals working in the field. Trainees' attitudes towards certain service user groups influence both the choice of specialty pursued and the therapeutic relationship (Benham 1988). Promoting the participation of individuals with ID in training activities may be especially valuable in helping mould trainees' attitudes, reducing negative emotions, providing a positive experience of working with this group and helping them to feel more skilled. Enriching the experiences of professionals during placements in ID is therefore an important step in both attracting individuals to this specialty and retaining their involvement.

Within the field's psychiatry and psychology, the development of formal networks of professionals working in ID has had a profound effect in terms of the recognition of the need for training, its formal inclusion on the training agenda, the availability of training opportunities and the develop-ment of clinical care standards and coherent national strategies. Training activities across different professional groups will help to improve aware-ness of mental health issues in ID and this could be instrumental in pro-moting special interest groups within other professions. Potentially, such special interest groups are a powerful vehicle for developing more effective services in terms of increasing the cohesion of service responses, raising treatment standards and improving clinical care.

TRAINING MENTAL HEALTH PROFESSIONALS

Diversity in the nature of mental health service provision for individuals with ID implies that a range of health care professionals and support staff require specialist knowledge. This is necessary to ensure that the mental health needs of individuals with ID living in the community are effectively identified, assessed, treated and managed. Within the fields of psychiatry and psychology, the profile of mental health problems in individuals with ID has grown, the need for specialist knowledge has been acknowledged and it is now formally included in professional training for psychiatrists. For many other mental health professionals, however, there is a lack of recognition of the need for formalised training in mental health and ID and training programmes are *ad hoc*.

Training in ID for psychiatrists

In the UK 'Psychiatry of ID' is concerned with the prevention, diagnosis and treatment of mental health problems in people with ID. Psychiatrists specialising in ID work in a variety of settings (e.g. hospitals, community residential homes, people's homes) and require expertise in a range of areas including paediatrics, neurology, epilepsy, genetics, biochemistry and psychology. The nature of this role necessitates close working relationships with a wide range of professionals (e.g. psychologists, nurses, psychotherapists, speech and language therapists, support staff) and family carers.

Since 2005, all postgraduate medical education and training across the UK has been governed by the Postgraduate Medical Education and Training Board (PMETB). The PMETB is independent of the government and is responsible for the standards and quality assurance of all postgraduate education, training and assessment in medicine and dentistry. Modernising Medical Careers (MMC) provides the structure for postgraduate medical education and incorporates a foundation period followed by specialty and general practice training programmes. The 'foundation programme' lasts for two years and is hospital-based. It is aimed at improving and expanding generic and acute care skills and comprises a curriculum with learning outcomes. Eligibility for full registration with the GMC is possible following completion of Year 1. Foundation posts in psychiatry have now been created by most National Health trusts and deaneries, although the number varies geographically. The second foundation year (FY2) provides opportunities for trainees to gain experience of working in different specialties. FY2 posts in psychiatry do not at present count towards specialist training, but this is currently under review.

Specialist training in psychiatry lasts for six years, divided into three years of core training (CT1–3) and three years of specialty training (ST4–6). During core training, 'core trainees' develop skills in various aspects of psychiatry. Workplace-, knowledge- and competency-based assessments, based on *Good Medical Practice* (GMC) and *Good Psychiatric Practice* (RCP), occur throughout the training period. On completion, core trainees complete the MRCPsych examination. This exam includes questions and cases in the psychiatry of ID and recent innovations include the participation of people with ID in the curriculum as trainers.

Specialisation begins in the fourth year when trainees become 'specialty registrars'. The suitability of trainees is assessed via a combination of portfolio from FY2, CV-based questions, a structured interview and assessment of teamwork and empathy. In order to further develop diagnostic, therapeutic and management skills, trainees complete clinical work, attend weekly academic meetings, gain teaching experience, conduct an original research project, serve on committees and participate in clinical audit. Higher training leads to one of six 'certificates of completion of training' (CCTs), one of which is the psychiatry of ID. On completion of training all psychiatrists are expected to have basic knowledge and competence in all psychiatric sub-specialties, including ID. It takes three years to gain a CCT in the Psychiatry of ID, of which one year can be spent in general psychiatry or another appropriate psychiatric specialty. Dual training programmes, lasting four to five years, are also possible where a trainee gains a CCT in the Psychiatry of ID and another specialty such as General Adult Psychiatry.

Other opportunities for psychiatrists to further their expertise in relation to ID also exist. Recently, the Royal College of Psychiatrists has redeveloped Continuing Professional Development (CPD) which requires psychiatrists to maintain, develop and remedy any knowledge and skill deficits. Participation in CPD is central to maintaining standards within clinical governance. Personal Development Plans (PDPs) enable psychiatrists to record evidence of the steps undertaken to assess, define, test with peers and achieve CPD objectives. The 'CPD Online' website provides comprehensive online training support for mental health professionals across the world. It consists of a growing selection of learning modules using different forms of media. Modules relating to Psychiatry of ID (Learning disability, DVLA and mental illness, Challenging behaviour, Sensory impairment and ID) are currently under development.

Also, within the Royal College of Psychiatry, the Faculty of the Psychiatry of ID aims to expand the knowledge of its members in this field and to develop policy that promotes the well-being of people with ID. Reflecting the changing circumstances within which the Faculty operates, its nature and role is fluid with sub-groups and working parties emerging to tackle specific issues such as the 'Interface between ID and old age psychiatry' and the 'Involvement of users and carers'. The Faculty organises a range of national conferences and consultation workshops, and acts as a valuable source of information for professionals and public alike. The Faculty has regional representatives and members in other committees within the Royal College. Interface working is a crucial aspect of the Faculty's work, helping to ensure that the interests of individuals with ID remain visible both within psychiatry and to other professional groups. For example, joint training events with the Old Age Faculty and joint working groups with the British Psychological Society have recently been organised. Such activities are vital in keeping the ID agenda in focus and ensuring a coherent professional stance in relation to policy developments.

Training in ID for clinical psychologists

In order to become Chartered, psychologists undertake a postgraduate three-year university course leading to a doctoral degree in Clinical

Psychology, approved by the British Psychological Society (BPS). Under the direct supervision of approved senior professional staff, trainees follow an academic programme which includes lectures on ID encompassing development; causes and characteristics; aspects of care (assessment and monitoring, interventions, skills development); service issues (normalisation, staff support, service provision) and organisation and policy (Powell et al. 1993). In addition to lectures, students learn research skills and must carry out a clinically relevant piece of original research. Academic teaching is integrated with periods of practical clinical experience in a variety of service specialties and across the full age spectrum. Trainees may opt to complete a six-month clinical placement in ID services. Hence, clinical exposure to individuals with ID is often optional and more likely to be gained following qualification.

Akin to developments within psychiatry, the BPS also provides opportunities for psychologists to expand their knowledge and skills in relation to the mental health needs of individuals with ID. Within the BPS, the Faculty of ID (FacID) provides a forum for psychologists with an interest in working with individuals with ID. The Faculty aims to encourage the exchange of information, ideas and expertise and to foster effective psychological services for this group. Faculty activities range from organising conferences and training events to liaising with other agencies and professional groups. This group also plays an important role in ensuring that the needs of individuals with ID are highlighted within psychology, across other health care professions and at a policy level. The BPS has a mandatory requirement for all chartered psychologists to maintain and enhance their professional skills. Therefore, CPD also plays a key role in expanding the knowledge and skills of psychologists in relation to individuals with ID. Through the Division of Clinical Psychology (DCP), the Faculty ID is responsible for a range of workshops and training events that form part of the CPD programme.

Training in ID for other mental health professionals

In addition to psychiatrists and psychologists, a broad range of other therapists also support individuals with ID and mental health problems. These include psychotherapists, challenging behaviour therapists, and art and play therapists. Therapists encompass a broad group, representing a variety of professional backgrounds, training and qualifications. Indeed, the titles under which therapists work may vary according to the context in which they work and differences are evident even within the same job title. For example, a psychotherapist may be a psychiatrist, social worker, psychologist or other mental health professional with further specialist training in psychotherapy. Increasingly, however, psychotherapists do not have backgrounds in these fields but have undertaken in-depth training in this area. Generalisations about the provision of mental health training for therapists in relation in individuals with ID are therefore problematic.

Across the UK, a broad range of organisations provide training programmes for therapists accredited by independent regulatory bodies. For example, psychotherapy qualifications may be accredited, although not exclusively, by the UK Council for Psychotherapy (UKCP) and the British Association of Psychotherapists. Arts therapy qualifications, including art, drama and music therapy, are governed by the Health Professions Council (HPC). Typically, courses are a mixture of practical and theoretical training methods. Although the majority of trainees receive lectures relating to individuals with ID, the inclusion of mental health as a topic within ID is not mandatory. The inclusion of mental health in ID, together with its form and content, is therefore determined at an institutional level and varies from course to course. Specialist ID lecturers often have a degree of autonomy in determining the content of lectures. For example, one lecturer in art therapy reported that she implicitly includes the mental, physical and emotional health agenda for adults with ID as well as the social context, policy and legislation for both in-patient and community health settings. Another reported including headings on emotional and mental health issues such as 'loss', 'abuse', 'trauma', 'secondary handicap' and 'attachment difficulties'.

Akin to many other mental health professionals, exposure to working with people with ID and mental health problems is most likely to occur during optional clinical placements. These take place in a variety of settings under the supervision of qualified practitioners. Post-qualification and continuing professional development also represent a valuable avenue for training in this area. Many of the governing bodies for therapists, such as the British Association of Art Therapists, recognise the need for a specific focus on mental health and ID and have facilitated the development of special interest groups. As is the case within psychiatry, such groups have been active in providing training opportunities, organising conferences and devising specific guidelines in relation to people with ID.

In recent years a wealth of educational and training resources has emerged to meet the need for specialised training in this area. Academic textbooks and distance learning tools, focusing on this topic and targeting specific groups are now widely available. A broad range of related training events, national and international conferences, provided by bodies such as the Royal Society of Medicine's Forum on Intellectual Disability, the Royal College of General Practitioners Learning Disability Working Group and university departments, are also routinely offered.

Training programmes, ranging from day-long workshops to academic courses, are also available for the broad range of practitioners working in ID services. Often, programme providers represent partnerships between clinicians working within NHS settings, academic institutions and service users. Such collaboration helps to ensure that training reflects clinical guidelines, current policy, local need and the views of people with ID using services. For example, the Estia Centre (Bouras and Holt 2001) in South East London works closely with local clinicians from a range of services, such as Community ID Teams and in-patient services, to provide a multi-disciplinary academic programme aimed specifically at supporting local practitioners. The Estia Centre is a training, research and development unit focusing on the mental health needs of adults with ID. The programme is held monthly and begins with a case presentation, usually of an individual presenting with complex needs and challenges. The presentation offers an opportunity for other clinicians to contribute ideas on the individual's treatment and management. This is followed by a review of recent policy and publications. With an ever-growing plethora of policies, it is vital that professionals are kept up to date with practice, law and changing responsibilities, an example being the Mental Capacity Act 2005: Deprivation of Liberty Safeguards (Office of the Public Guardian 2008). The programme concludes with an invited speaker, renowned in their own area, who delivers a presentation on a subject related to mental health and ID. Recent presentations have included:

- psychotherapy and people with ID
- bereavement, loss and ageing
- family therapy and people with ID
- psychiatric services for adolescents and adults with Asperger's syndrome and autistic-spectrum disorders
- the new Mental Health Act.

Undergraduate and postgraduate courses are now available for a wide range of professionals working with people with ID and additional mental health problems. This includes social workers, nurses, therapists, psychology graduates, and residential service managers. Examples include the Tizard Centre, based at the University of Kent, which offers a range of short courses together with BSc, MA and MSc in Intellectual and Developmental Disabilities. The Norah Fry Research Centre at the University of Bristol has recently launched a new MSc programme called 'Inclusive theory and practice: Empowering people with learning disabilities' comprising three phases (postgraduate certificate, postgraduate diploma and master's degree), each of which can be taken independently or in succession. The Institute of Psychiatry (IoP) and the Estia Centre developed the

MSc Mental Health in Learning Disabilities (MHiLD) (www.mentalhealth-studies.iop.kcl.ac.uk) in 1999. It has grown significantly in strength over the years and is nationally and internationally recognised as a leading qualification in the field. The MSc in MHiLD is part of the Mental Health Studies Programme within the division of Psychological Medicine at the IoP.

The MSc in MHiLD is designed to provide continuing professional development for mental health professionals as well as up-to-date knowledge and understanding of mental health issues for psychology graduates with academic and/or clinical interests in the area. The MSc consists of five modules: basic mental health, research methods, two specialist ID modules and a dissertation. The specialist modules cover: aetiology, psychopathology and assessment; theoretical and empirical basis of clinical management of the mental health needs; forensic issues and services; neuro-developmental aspects; pervasive developmental disorders. The programme is delivered by a diverse range of visiting lecturers – academic and clinical experts in MHiLD – to complement the core IoP teaching staff. Links with active research groups at the IoP have also been established so students can undertake their MSc dissertation under the supervision of experienced clinical/academic researchers.

TRAINING INITIATIVES TO DEVELOP COMPETENCE OF SUPPORT STAFF AND FAMILY CARERS

It is essential that people with ID are supported by family carers and/or support staff and health/social care professionals that are competent in promoting positive mental health, identifying mental health problems and accessing/providing appropriate services and intervention.

Support staff

People with ID who do not live with their families or independently are often in receipt of support from paid staff (commonly referred to as 'support staff'). They provide support in a range of ways, such as in staffed group homes, or visiting individuals in their private residence for a few hours a day (referred to as 'outreach support'). In a 2005 audit there were over 35,000 adults with ID living in supported residential care in England (Health and Social Care Information Centre 2005). Additionally 58,000 people with ID in the UK use day services (www.mencap.org.uk 2008).

Mental health problems can be difficult to detect in people with ID. Eliciting psychopathology relies heavily on an individual being able to describe their inner world. Communication impairments are common among people with ID (Taylor 2009) and they may not be able to describe their inner world, thus important indicators of mental ill health (i.e. delusions, hallucinations, subjective mood) may not be identified. Support staff may misinterpret objective signs of mental ill health (i.e. changes in behaviour) and attribute them to the person's disability and not consider seeking help. It is vital that support staff have adequate training in mental health needs, as they play a vital role in mental health care, such as initial recognition of a problem, referral to services and supporting the assessment, treatment and recovery process.

In recent years it has been recognised that support staff often have no formal qualifications in health or social care but are given the role of providing some of the most important aspects of maintaining a person's quality of life. In 2001, a new national policy was published for people with ID in England, 'Valuing People' (Department of Health 2001). It introduced the concept of formal vocational qualifications specific to people with ID. This led to the development of the Learning Disability Awards Framework, which for the first time implemented compulsory standards for social care staff, in the form of an 'Induction Award'. This award provided support staff with an overview of values and rights of people using services, national policy and statutory requirements such as vulnerable adults and health and safety. Staff are then required to enrol on further training such as National Vocational Qualifications (NVQs), which may or may not include mental health.

In South East London a training programme has been specifically developed to address the skills and knowledge gap that exists in meeting the mental health needs of people with ID. The programme was developed by the Estia Centre (Bouras and Holt 2001) in close collaboration with local clinical services and serves three inner city boroughs with a population of over 750,000. The area has high levels of poverty and a diverse ethnic population. It is estimated that over 3,000 people with ID are known to services. A range of services are commissioned by the Primary Care Trusts and Social Services, including over 100 not for profit organisations offering supported housing, outreach services, day and employment services.

In developing its training programme the Estia Centre initially completed a training needs analysis with local service providers. Local groups of people with ID and professionals from the local Community ID Teams were also consulted. This resulted in a rolling programme of workshops that are provided free to local not-for-profit services.

Workshops are developed with input from a range of disciplines and from people using services. Content reflects the evidence base of the subject and current policy. Workshops are based around a framework of skills and knowledge that participants should possess to provide effective care. Table 8.1 shows the framework that was developed for the Mental Health in ID Workshop.

TABLE 8.1

Skills and knowledge framework on which mental health workshops are developed and delivered for different care settings

Type of staff/service	Skills and knowledge
Level 1: Support staff working in social care housing	1. Recognise that people with ID can develop mental health problems 2. Identify factors that increase/decrease vulnerability to mental health problems 3. Develop proactive plans with the individual to reduce vulnerability 4. Recognise, monitor and report changes in behaviour that could be associated with the development of a mental health problem 5. Aware of local access for assessment and treatment of mental health problems 6. Contribute to the assessment process by providing accurate information about history, normal, current and changes in functioning/behaviour, possible symptoms, recent life events 7. Effectively prepare and support the individual through the assessment process, with a particular focus on enabling communication 8. Aware of the Mental Capacity legislation and their role/responsibilities within it
Level 2: Support staff working in social care housing who work with individuals who have identified mental health problems	Including all listed in Level 1. 1. Knowledge of the individual's diagnosis and its presentation 2. Contribute to and implement individual intervention packages and monitor/report on progress 3. Support the individual in understanding their mental health problem, and intervention plan 4. Comprehensive understanding of risk factors for relapse and develop proactive strategies to reduce their likelihood and/or impact 5. Ability to recognise early signs of relapse 6. Promote the recovery and social inclusion of the individual 7. Knowledge and involvement in care planning processes (i.e. Care Programme Approach in England)
Level 3: Health care assistants/support staff working in specialist assessment and treatment services	Including all listed in Levels 1 and 2. 1. Comprehensive knowledge of the roles and responsibilities of the multidisciplinary team and external agencies/professionals working into the service 2. De-escalate and manage violent/aggression situations 3. Make accurate observations of individuals identified as at risk 4. Knowledge of the Mental Health legislation and their role/responsibilities within it 5. In-depth knowledge of the environment's security policies and procedures

The Estia Centre offers an increasing number of workshops around mental health and associated issues, including:

- Activity and Skills Development
- Mental Capacity Act (2005)
- Contribute to the Management of Substance Use and Misuse in People with ID
- Introduction to Autism
- Introduction to Challenging Needs
- Mental Health and People with ID
- Mental Health and Older People with ID
- Risk Around an Individual
- Risk Assessment and Management for Senior Staff
- Self-Injurious Behaviour
- Using Objects, Photos and Symbols as Aids to Communication
- Independence for People with ID

Any of the above workshops can be tailored to the needs of a particular staff team. Workshops are also specifically designed around the needs of individual people using local services, and clinicians are always fully involved. On average the Estia Centre delivers 80 workshop days per annum attended by 800 staff.

Many of the materials used in the programme are taken from *Mental Health in Learning Disabilities: A Training Resource* (Holt et al. 2005), which was developed by the Estia Centre. It is a comprehensive programme, consisting of over 70 hours of learning activities, which are split into 18 themed modules. It provides trainers with detailed lecture notes, slides, handouts, various learning activities and video case vignettes. Trainers are also provided with an accompanying reader, which gives detailed supporting information for each module. The training resource has been extremely successful and is in its third edition. It has been translated into five languages.

The Centre has produced other publications for support staff in the form of guidance. *Supporting Complex Needs* (Hardy et al. 2006) is a practical guide produced in collaboration with the charity Turning Point. It provides a proactive approach to meeting mental health needs, empowering support staff to recognise their own valued role in implementing high-quality support for people using services. Challenging behaviour often results in high levels of stress for support staff and in reduced opportunities for people with ID. *Keeping it Together* (Woodward et al. 2007) is a self-help guide, supporting staff to build their own skills in developing strategies to support those whose behaviour is challenging. It offers realistic information and guidance on how to work with other professionals. Both people who use services and support staff were involved in the development of these publications.

Family Carers

It is estimated that 60% of adults with ID live with their families (Department of Health 2001), though there is little published evidence about enhancing their knowledge and skills in relation to the mental health of their family member. Several charitable organisations (e.g., Foundation for People with Learning Disabilities, Down's Syndrome Association) have produced booklets educating carers on recognising mental health problems and promoting well-being. In 2004 the Royal College of Psychiatrists launched a campaign for carers of those with mental health problems, and this resulted in a number of short publications, including one directed at carers of people with ID.

An example of a comprehensive initiative was the publication of *Guide to Mental Health for Families and Carers of People with Intellectual Disabilities* (Holt et al. 2004). The guide was developed in consultation with family carers and people with ID. It focused on what people wanted to know in regard to their family members' mental health, how to recognise possible mental health problems, how and when to access services, the range of available treatments and how carers can help themselves. Case vignettes were used to illustrate how mental health problems can affect the individual with ID but also the difficulties and dilemmas that carers face. The guide was formally evaluated with carers, who found that it was relevant, easily accessible and offered most of the information they required (Gratsa et al. 2007).

In regard to education programmes, there are anecdotal examples of seminars and presentations, but no published material or evidence on more formal programmes.

THE WAY FORWARD FOR EFFECTIVE TRAINING OF SUPPORT STAFF

Although the provision of mental health training is an important step in ensuring that staff have the appropriate skills and in improving access to mental health services, relatively few staff currently receive any training. In the absence of a national strategy focusing on mental health issues, the availability and content of training is mostly *ad hoc*, and it is typically provided in-house. Consequently, there is a lack of information about the nature of available training and a paucity of evidence about its effectiveness. Yet demonstrating the outcomes of training for individuals with ID, for professionals, staff and carers is vital in ensuring its place on the training agenda. Focusing predominantly on residential support staff and carers, this section examines research evidence about the impact of training initiatives and its role in improving staff awareness of mental health problems. Gaps in knowledge concerning the role of training for professionals, in changing staff behaviour and improving the mental health of individuals with ID are highlighted. Finally, some recommendations are made for the delivery of training for support staff at national and local levels.

Is training effective?

Research in several areas of ID demonstrates a positive relationship between training, knowledge, confidence and staff performance (Allen at al. 1997; Hames 1996). However, evidence about the outcomes of training in respect of mental health is lacking and significant gaps in the knowledge base exist. For example, there is little if any evidence about the impact of specialist training for clinicians. A small number of studies report an association between mental health training and increased clinician knowledge. For example, in the USA, Loschen and Kirchner (1998) described the development of a curriculum in mental health and ID dual diagnosis using 'problem based learning' (Loschen 1997). This comprised 20 hours of didactic training, divided into eight sessions, plus an additional 20 hours of practice within a clinical setting. A total of 12 clinicians reported that the quality of the training was adequate and the experience had a positive impact on their knowledge and practice. Although the training was also designed for care staff, this group did not evaluate the materials.

Similarly, Gibbs and Priest (1999) evaluated a diploma module aimed at increasing the knowledge of ID nurses in relation to mental health problems. The training comprised ten three-hour taught sessions and reflective diary work focusing on applying theory to practice. Participants reported that the training changed their perspective towards mental health problems and enhanced their knowledge, skills and attitudes ($n = 30$). With a follow-up period ranging from 6 to 18 months, a smaller subset of the sample reported that the training had a positive impact on their practice. Measuring knowledge of psychopathology more directly by using the Mini PAS-ADD (Prosser et al. 1997) as a comparator, Quigley et al. (2001) conducted a postal survey of 116 health and social care staff working in ID services. They reported low levels of knowledge about symptoms, but found that trained staff had significantly greater knowledge and greater confidence in supporting individuals with mental health problems, compared to untrained staff. However, the nature and quality of the training received was not explored. Only one randomised controlled study ($n = 84$) investigating the efficacy of a mental health in ID curriculum for care staff was evident. Conducted by Mester (1999) in the USA, the study reported that compared to untrained staff, staff attending a two-day workshop had significantly improved knowledge and problem-solving skills relating to mental health problems in people with ID.

Thus, studies have often relied on participants' perceptions to measure the impact of training on knowledge. Measuring the impact of training on staff awareness more directly, Costello (2005) conducted a quasi-experimental study to examine the impact of an introductory mental health training workshop on staff knowledge of psychopathology, attitudes towards mental health professionals and referral decisions ($n = 131$). Based on the training package 'Mental Health in Learning Disabilities' (Bouras and Holt 1997), the study raised concerns about the criteria used by staff to judge the presence of mental health problems (Costello et al. 2007). As in previous research (Mester 1999; Quigley et al. 2001), using pre- and post-training questionnaires the study found evidence to suggest that training was associated with increased knowledge of psychopathology. In addition, training improved staff attitudes towards mental health services and increased the likelihood of referral decisions. Improvements in awareness were maintained, with significant increases in knowledge, attitudes and referral practice evident four months after the delivery of training. Tsiantis et al. (2004) and Holt et al. (2000) reported similar findings using the same training materials with care staff from institutional and community settings in Greece ($n = 36$) and Austria ($n = 36$) respectively.

Of course, there can be no guarantee that increased staff knowledge of mental health issues gained through training will be translated into better practice such as more accurate referral decisions. To date, no studies have measured the effects of mental health training on behaviour in practice. As such, the impact of training initiatives on clinician performance, on the pathway to care and on the mental health of individuals with ID remains uncertain. A conceptual model for understanding staff responses to mental health problems and for predicting how training may influence staff behaviour has yet to be developed. For example, a range of variables influence the care pathway. Among others, these include staff awareness, the formal and informal culture of the setting in which the mental health problem occurs, the experience of gatekeepers such as managers and GPs, and the availability of services. The manner in which these factors inter-relate to determine staff behaviour has not been investigated. More evidence about the nature and relative role of factors influencing the assessment and referral process is therefore required to build theoretical models of staff behaviour and to identify the mechanisms underpinning effective training. As demonstrated in the field of challenging behaviour (e.g. Hastings and Remington 1994), examining the cognitive processes underpinning referral decisions, such as documenting the causal attributions of a range of mental health problems, may be fruitful in achieving some progress towards this goal.

Recommendations for the delivery of training for support staff

This section makes recommendations for the development of training both strategically at a national level and locally for individual organisations aiming to improve the effectiveness of the services they provide for people with ID and mental health problems. Three key areas are considered. These relate to infrastructure (e.g. management support, resources, staff time), training materials (e.g. quality, flexibility) and good practice dissemination (e.g. nationally agreed standards).

A. Infrastructure

- An infrastructure is necessary to support training, including national standards of care for people with ID and mental health problems to drive accreditation and certification of course, together with secure career paths.
- Use of well-established training departments with experience and resources. This is difficult for small organisations, with a dispersed staff group, to replicate. One solution is to use commercial organisations, with staff attending training activities held on a national level, or to use the services of such an organisation in-house.
- Training care staff alone is an ineffective strategy for producing change. Training must be provided within a context of a supportive management system that provides staff with clear models in terms of first-line managers acting as 'practice leaders'.
- Including managers in training activities is vital. It allows them to share a knowledge base with their staff, and to set up processes that facilitate the continued development of issues identified by the training.
- Supervised practical training is vital to transfer, strengthen and maintain positive changes at work.
- Releasing staff for training and maintaining service quality. To safeguard training it is suggested that the requirement for a specified amount of training in designated areas should be written into the contracts drawn up between the commissioners and providers of services.

B. Training materials

- Training materials must be flexible so that they can be used by staff groups independently in their own settings.
- The materials should be attractive, easy to understand and presented in a variety of formats. This helps to keep people interested, and we all have our own preferences for the way in which we learn. Some

prefer lectures, others small group discussions, others visual material and so on.

- The material presented should be relevant to the staff team, building on the skills they already have, while addressing their anxieties and areas of weakness. For example, 'problem-based learning' gives staff a framework for solving problems and enables them to use the knowledge gained in an academic setting more effectively in the workplace.
- Information must be conveyed in a meaningful way. For instance, people do not present with a diagnostic label such as 'schizophrenia'. Rather, they usually present with disturbed behaviour, indicative of a range of possible causes. Simply providing staff with lectures on distinct psychiatric disorders, therefore, may not be helpful. Using case studies and real workplace issues helps staff to learn how to gather relevant information in line with mental health assessment and diagnostic formulation.
- Designing training around particular individuals is useful. For instance, a morning spent considering various aspects of autistic spectrum disorders followed by an afternoon working with a staff team developing ways together as to how to work with a specific individual with this diagnosis.
- Enriching the training experience is important for improving the recruitment and retention of staff in mental health and ID. Careful consideration is needed to ensure that training is not an aversive experience. Promoting the participation of individuals with ID in training activities may be especially valuable in shaping attitudes, reducing negative emotions, providing a positive experience of working with this group and helping staff to feel more skilled.

C. Good practice dissemination

- Where possible, training must adhere to agreed national standards.
- Good practice needs to be disseminated. For example, the participation of individuals with ID as trainers in the education of medical students and psychiatrists is a promising development, which warrants replication in the training of other professional groups.

CONCLUSION

Overall, training in ID struggles at many different levels. Given their key role in the process of deinstitutionalisation, the greatest progress in the provision of specialist training is evident within psychiatry and psychology. However, currently training in mental health and ID is mandatory only for trainee psychiatrists. For other groups, clinical exposure to individuals with ID and mental health problems is optional and more likely to be gained following qualification. Additional training focusing on this topic is mostly available through CPD or through the establishment of forums comprising therapists with a special interest in this area.

Access to specialist knowledge is a fundamental step in improving the ability of support staff and family carers to provide effective support. Policy initiatives, such as Valuing People (Department of Health 2001), which introduced the Learning Disability Awards Framework (LDAF), emphasise generic rather than specialist skills. Mental Health and Challenging Behaviour are only optional topics of the LDAF, providing basic knowledge and amounting to approximately one hour and a quarter of staff time. The ambitious targets prescribed by this strategy require a substantial level of service resources to be directed towards achieving the mandatory elements of the LDAF. Together with the omission of a time scale for completion of optional units of the training strategy, it is probable that future resources for mental health training will be diminished. The impact of such initiatives for improving access to mental health services is therefore unclear.

It is essential that the structure of training facilitates and reflects the multidisciplinary nature of this work. Hence, providing professionals and carers with a common language and framework is an integral function of the training process. Enriching training experiences is also important in respect of recruitment and retention in the field of mental health and ID. Training activities may be instrumental in the formation of networks able to influence positively the standards of care and national strategies. Ultimately, a more systematic co-ordinated approach on a national basis is needed. At present, the principal responsibility for training rests with the departments of psychiatry, child health, family and community medicine. At a postgraduate level, teaching in ID remains *ad hoc* and essentially dependent on the interests and enthusiasms of individual health professionals, primary health physicians, local service providers and postgraduate training departments.

Nevertheless, some progress in raising the profile of mental health problems in individuals with ID on the training agenda is evident. Educational materials, such as academic textbooks and distance learning tools, focusing on this topic and targeting specific groups are now widely available. A broad range of related training events, national and international conferences are routinely offered and examples of good training practice are also apparent. For example, the Estia Centre has pioneered a number of groundbreaking initiatives and delivers a comprehensive training programme for a range of staff working in ID services. For further information on this work at an international level, see Chapter 3.

NECESSARY STEPS TO BETTER SERVICES

- Currently, training in mental health and ID is mandatory only for psychiatrists. This topic should be formally included in the curriculum of a broader range of mental health professionals.
- Individuals with ID and additional mental health problems require support from a wide range of professionals, support staff and family carers. Training must facilitate and reflect the multidisciplinary nature of this work and provide a common language and framework.
- Enriching training experiences is an important aspect of recruitment and retention.
- Training activities may be instrumental in the formation of networks able to influence positively the standards of care and national strategies. Currently, there is a lack of evidence about the impact of training. More evidence about the nature and relative role of factors influencing the assessment and referral process is required to build theoretical models of staff behaviour and to identify the mechanisms underpinning effective training.

REFERENCES

Allen, D., McDonald, L., Dunn, C. and Doyle, T. (1997) Changing care staff approaches to the prevention and management of aggressive behaviour in a residential treatment unit for persons with mental retardation and challenging behaviour. *Research in Developmental Disabilities*, 18, 101–112.

Benham, P.K. (1988) Attitudes of occupational therapy personnel towards persons with disabilities. *American Journal of Occupational Therapy*, 42, 305–311.

Bouras, N. and Holt, G. (eds) (1997) *A Training Package for Staff Working with People with a Dual Diagnosis of Learning Disability and a Mental Health Problem* (2nd ed.). Brighton, UK: Pavilion Publishing.

Bouras, N. and Holt, G. (2001) Community mental health services for adults with learning disabilities. In G. Thornicroft and G. Szmukler (eds), *Textbook of Community Psychiatry*. Oxford, UK: Oxford University Press.

Costello, H. (2005) *Does training carers improve outcome for adults with learning disabilities and mental health problems?* PhD Thesis, Institute of Psychiatry–King's College London, University of London.

Costello, H., Bouras, N. and Davis, H. (2007) The role of training in improving community care staff awareness of mental health problems in people with intellectual disabilities. *Journal of Applied Research in Intellectual Disabilities*, 20, 228–235.

Department of Health (2001) *Valuing People: A New Strategy for Learning Disability in the 21st Century*. London: HMSO.

Department of Health (2007) *Services for People with Learning Disabilities and Challenging Behaviour or Mental Health Needs*. London: HMSO.

Gibbs, M. and Priest, H.M. (1999) Designing and implementing a 'dual diagnosis' module: A review of the literature and some preliminary findings. *Nurse Education Today*, 19, 357–363.

Graham, S., Herbert, R., Price, S. and Williams, S. (2004) Attitudes and emotions of trainees in learning disability psychiatry. *Psychiatric Bulletin*, 28, 254–256.

Gratsa, A., Spiller, M.J., Holt, G., Joyce, T., Hardy, S. and Bouras, N. (2007) Developing a mental health guide for families and carers of people with intellectual disabilities. *Journal of Applied Research in Intellectual Disabilities*, 20, 77–86.

Hames, A. (1996) The effects of experience and sexual abuse training on the attitudes of learning disability. *Journal of Intellectual Disability Research*, 40, 544–549.

Hardy, S., Kramer, R., Holt, G., Woodward, P. and Chaplin, E. (2006) *Supporting Complex Needs: A Practical Guide for Support Staff Working with People with a Learning Disability Who Have Mental Health Needs*. London: Turning Point.

Hastings, R. and Remington, B. (1994) Rules of engagement: Towards an analysis of staff responses to challenging behaviour. *Research in Developmental Disabilities*, 15, 279–298.

Health and Social Care Information Centre (2005) *Community Care Statistics 2005, Supported Residents (Adults), England*. London: NHS Health and Social Care Information Centre.

Holt, G., Costello, H., Bouras, N., Diareme, S., Hillery, J., Moss, S. et al. (2000) BIOMED-MEROPE Project: Service provision for adults with mental retardation: A European perspective. *Journal of Intellectual Disability Research*, 44, 685–696.

Holt, G., Gratsa, A., Bouras, N., Joyce, T., Spiller, M.J. and Hardy, S. (2004) *Guide to Mental Health for Families and Carers of People with Intellectual Disabilities*. London: Jessica Kinglsey.

Holt, G., Hardy, S. and Bouras, N. (2005) *Mental Health in Learning Disabilities: A Training Resource*. Brighton, UK: Pavilion Publishing.

Loschen, E.L. (1997) Problem-based learning curriculum: An alternative curriculum for the basic sciences. *Educaceo Medica*, 2, 14–20.

Loschen, E.L. and Kirchner, L.C. (1998) Using problem-based learning in staff training for individuals with a dual diagnosis. *NADD Bulletin*, 1, 43–46.

Mester, C.S. (1999) Efficacy of a curriculum on dual diagnosis for direct care personnel. *NADD Bulletin*, 1, 107–112.

Office of the Public Guardian (2008) *Mental Capacity Act 2005: Deprivation of Liberty Safeguards*. London: The Stationery Office.

Powell, G.E., Young, R. and Frosh, S. (1993) (eds) *Curriculum in Clinical Psychology*. Leicester, UK: British Psychological Society Publications.

Prosser, H., Moss, S., Costello, H. and Simpson, N. (1997) *The Mini PAS-ADD: An Assessment Schedule for the Detection of Mental Health Problems in Adults with Learning Disability (Mental Retardation)*. Manchester, UK: Hester Adrian Research Centre, University of Manchester.

Quigley, A., Murray, G.C., McKenzie, K. and Elliot, G. (2001) Staff knowledge about symptoms of mental health in people with learning disabilities. *Journal of Learning Disabilities*, 5, 235–244.

Taylor, C. (2009) The assessment of communication in people with learning disabilities. *Advances in Mental Health and Learning Disabilities*, 2, 4.

Tsiantis, J., Diareme, S., Dimitrakaki, C., Kolaitis, G., Flios, A., Christogiorgos, S. et al. (2004) Care staff awareness training on mental health needs of adults with learning disabilities: Results from a Greek sample. *Journal of Learning Disabilities*, 8 (3), 221–234.

Woodward, P., Hardy, S. and Joyce, T. (2007) *Keeping It Together: A Guide for Support Staff Working with People Whose Behaviour is Challenging*. Brighton, UK: Pavilion Publishing.

Online resources

- American Association on Intellectual and Developmental Disabilities (AAIDD): www.aamr.org
- Association of European Psychiatrists Neuroimaging Section: www.aep.lu/about/sections/Neuroimaging%20Section/index%20neuroimaging.html
- Australasian Society for the Study of Intellectual Disability: www.assid.org.au
- *The basics of MRI* – book by Joseph P. Hornak: www.cis.rit.edu/htbooks/mri/inside.htm
- Brain Image Analysis Unit: www.brainmap.co.uk
- British Institute of Learning Disabilities: www.bild.org.uk
- Centre for Neuroimaging Sciences: www.neuroimagingsciences.com
- Commission for Social Care Inspection: www.csci.org.uk
- Crime prevention: www.nacro.org.uk
- Department of Health: www.dh.gov.uk
- Estia Centre: www.estiacentre.org
- Forensic learning disability: www.ldoffenders.co.uk
- Forensic mental health care network: www.forensicnetwork.scot.nhs.uk/learning disabilities.asp
- Forensic psychiatry research: www.fprs.org
- Foundation for People with Learning Disabilities: www.learningdisabilities.org.uk
- Healthcare Commission: www.healthcarecommission.org.uk/homepage.cfm
- Home Office: www.homeoffice.gov.uk
- International Association for the Scientific Study of Intellectual Disabilities: www.iassid.org/iassid/index.php
- Judith Trust: www.judithtrust.org.uk

- Learning Disability Awards Framework: www.ldaf.org.uk
- Mencap: www.mencap.org.uk
- Ministry of Justice: www.justice.gov.uk
- Monitor: www.monitor-nhsft.gov.uk
- National Association for the Dually Diagnosed (NADD): www.thenadd.org
- People First: www.peoplefirst.org.uk
- Royal College of Psychiatrists: www.rcpsych.ac.uk
- Simply physics – 'The home of MRI physics put simply': www.simplyphysics. com
- Social Care Institute for Excellence (SCIE): www.scie.org.uk
- Social Exclusion Unit: www.socialexclusionunit.gov.uk
- Statistical Parametric Mapping: www.fil.ion.ucl.ac.uk/spm
- Tizard Centre: www.ukc.ac.uk/tizard
- Valuing People: www.valuingpeople.gov.uk
- Whole Brain Atlas: www.med.harvard.edu/AANLIB/home.htm
- World Health Organisation: www.who.int/en
- World Psychiatric Association: www.wpanet.org

Author index

Subject index

Locators in *italic* refer to illustrations. Locators in **bold** refer to significant content. Locators for headings which also have subheadings refer to general aspects of that topic.

146